THE
PARKAY MARGARINE
COOKBOOK

From Kraft

A Benjamin Company Book

Recipes and Editorial: The Kraft Kitchens
Photography and Art: Kraft, Inc. Creative Services

Copyright © 1980 Kraft, Inc.
ISBN 0-87502-074-7
Library of Congress Catalog Card Number 79-54946
All Rights Reserved
Published by The Benjamin Company, Inc.
485 Madison Avenue
New York, New York 10022

Printed in the United States of America
First Printing: April, 1980

Table Of Contents

PARKAY

Although margarine is considered a modern convenience food, its origin dates back to the nineteenth century. It was developed in 1869 by a French chemist, Hippolyte Mege-Mouries. At that time there was an economic need for an alternative to butter which was very scarce and expensive due to the Industrial Revolution and the Franco-Prussian War.

The new product named oleomargarine, made with less expensive animal fats, could be sold for an affordable price. Of course, the quality of the original oleo-margarine was no match for the high quality product we know today as margarine. Its popularity, however, spread throughout Europe and by 1874 manufacturing began in the United States.

Since dairy farming has always been a major agricultural industry in the United States, the introduction of margarine met with strong opposition. The Oleomargarine Act of 1886 was the first of a series of anti-margarine laws which continued until 1950. Heavy taxes were imposed and manufacturers and distributors required licensing. In addition, many state laws prohibited the sale or at least the coloring of margarine.

Despite these restrictions, innovative research continued to improve the product. Vegetable oils — first imported coconut oil and later domestic soy and cottonseed oils — replaced animal fat as the basic ingredient. To improve the nutritive value, margarine was fortified with vitamin A, an essential vitamin which occurs naturally in butter. Another advancement was the inclusion of a capsule or wafer of yellow food coloring which the homemaker could blend with the white margarine thereby making it more appetizing.

In 1941, the Food and Drug Administration issued a Standard of Identity for margarine which designated the amounts of required and optional ingredients in margarine and removed the "imitation butter" stigma. Several years later, the Margarine Act of 1950 repealed the restrictive federal taxes and fees. Due to these measures and the many product innovations, by the late 1960's consumers were buying twice as much margarine as butter.

Kraft entered the margarine market with Parkay margarine in 1937. This product was a natural outgrowth for the company because of its many oil-based products. During the last forty years, Kraft has been a major force and innovator in the manufacture of margarine. A major change was the development of Miracle brand margarine, a stick margarine which was spreadable at refrigerator temperature. More recent developments include a soft margarine, soft Parkay margarine, and a liquid margarine, Squeeze Parkay margarine. In 1970 "Country Fresh Flavor," a flavor blend of components closely duplicating those of butter, was added to all Kraft margarines.

This cookbook features an imaginative variety of recipes made with three major Parkay margarines — regular, soft and Squeeze — which range in consistency from semifirm to liquid. Each has its own characteristic cooking uses:

- Regular Parkay margarine in stick form is ideal for all general purpose cooking and baking. Use it in recipes that require creaming or cutting-in preparation such as for cookies, cakes, biscuits and pastry.

- Soft Parkay margarine blends quickly and smoothly with other ingredients; therefore, it is particularly suited to seasoned spreads for breads and appetizers, fillings and toppings.

- Squeeze Parkay margarine has many uses in recipes requiring melted margarine. It is excellent for quick mix breads, cakes, cookies and pancakes; sautéeing and oven frying; and seasoning vegetables.

These Kraft margarines offer qualities — versatility, convenience and reliability — that are well-suited to today's casual, fast-paced lifestyles. The recipes which were developed in the Kraft Kitchens include quick and easy ideas for weekly meals and more detailed specialties for the weekend gourmet. Family dining, instant meals and formal or informal entertaining — there is something for everyone and every occasion created for your cooking pleasure.

The Kraft Kitchens

Rising From The Bread Board

The marvelous aroma of fresh-from-the-oven bread has always evoked nostalgic memories of home, family, hospitality and love. With the renewed interest in yeast baking as a creative art and a relaxing pastime, that wonderful aroma of fresh bread is once again rising from the bread board.

Yeast Baking Basics

- Active dry yeast will keep several months in a cool dry place.

- Clear dry days are the best for yeast bread baking. Dough may become moist and sticky on hot humid days.

- Rising yeast dough should be covered with a clean damp cloth, waxed paper or inverted bowl and placed in a warm area (80° to 85° F).

- To knead, shape dough into a round ball on a floured surface. Slightly flatten the ball and fold in half toward you. Press the dough and push away with the heel of the hand. Rotate the dough a quarter turn and repeat the kneading process until the dough is smooth and elastic.

- The dough is "proofed" when it is double in volume and dome-shaped with small bubbles just below the surface. When the dough is pressed with a fingertip, a depression will remain.

- For a soft tender crust, brush bread or rolls with melted margarine just after removing from the oven.

- To freeze bread or rolls, cool thoroughly and wrap securely in aluminum foil or other moisture-vaporproof wrap. Before freezing, label the package indicating type of bread and date.

- Breads stored in the refrigerator become stale more quickly than those stored at room temperature or in the freezer.

- To reheat bread or rolls, wrap in aluminum foil and heat at 350°, 10 to 25 minutes depending on the size.

Apricot Ladder Loaves

1 cup dried apricots	1 egg
½ cup chopped nuts	½ teaspoon grated lemon rind
¼ cup packed brown sugar	* * *
1 teaspoon lemon juice	1 egg yolk
2½ to 3 cups flour	2 tablespoons milk
¼ cup granulated sugar	3 tablespoons flour
1 pkg. active dry yeast	1 tablespoon Parkay margarine,
1 teaspoon salt	melted
½ cup milk	1 tablespoon granulated sugar
Parkay margarine	¼ teaspoon cinnamon
¼ cup water	

Cook apricots in boiling water 15 minutes. Drain well; chop. Combine apricots, nuts, brown sugar and lemon juice; mix well. Cool. In large mixing bowl, combine 1 cup flour, granulated sugar, yeast and salt. Heat milk, ⅓ cup margarine and water over low heat until warm. Add to flour mixture; beat 3 minutes at medium speed of electric mixer. Add ½ cup flour, egg and lemon rind; beat 2 minutes at high speed. Stir in enough remaining flour to form a soft dough. On lightly floured surface, knead dough until smooth and elastic. Place in greased bowl; brush with melted margarine. Cover; let rise in warm place until double in volume, about 1½ hours. Punch down dough; divide in half. On lightly floured surface, roll out each half to 10 × 6-inch rectangle; spread half of apricot mixture lengthwise on center third of dough. Cut short strips at 1-inch intervals on both sides of filling. Crisscross the strips over filling. Place on greased cookie sheet. Repeat with remaining dough. Cover; let rise until double in volume, about 45 minutes.

Brush loaves with combined egg yolk and milk; sprinkle with combined flour, margarine, sugar and cinnamon. Bake at 350°, 25 to 30 minutes.

2 loaves

Swedish Tea Ring

2½ to 3 cups flour
¼ cup sugar
1 pkg. active dry yeast
1 teaspoon salt
½ cup milk
¼ cup water
  Parkay margarine
1 egg

¼ cup Parkay margarine,
  melted
½ cup raisins
¼ cup granulated sugar
¼ cup packed brown sugar
¼ cup chopped nuts
1 tablespoon cinnamon
  Vanilla Drizzle

*   *   *

In large mixing bowl, combine 1 cup flour, sugar, yeast and salt. Heat milk, water and ⅓ cup margarine over low heat until warm. Add to flour mixture; beat 3 minutes at medium speed of electric mixer. Add ½ cup flour and egg; beat 2 minutes at high speed. Stir in enough remaining flour to form a soft dough. On lightly floured surface, knead dough until smooth and elastic. Place in greased bowl; brush with melted margarine. Cover; let rise in warm place until double in volume, about 1½ hours. Punch down dough; let rest 10 minutes.

On lightly floured surface, roll out dough to 15 × 10-inch rectangle. Brush with margarine; sprinkle with combined raisins, sugars, nuts and cinnamon. Roll up, starting at long end; seal long end. Place on greased cookie sheet. Join ends to form ring; seal ends. With scissors, cut two-thirds of the way through ring at 1-inch intervals; turn each section on its side. Let rise until double in volume, about 45 minutes. Bake at 350°, 25 to 30 minutes. Drizzle with:

Vanilla Drizzle

1 cup sifted confectioners'
  sugar

1 tablespoon milk
1 teaspoon vanilla

Combine ingredients; mix well.

Regency Brunch Ring

1 13¾-oz. pkg. hot roll mix   1 cup sugar
1 tablespoon grated lemon rind   ¾ cup finely chopped nuts
½ cup Parkay margarine, melted   2 teaspoons cinnamon

Prepare hot roll mix as directed on package for basic dough, adding lemon rind with egg. Shape dough into 24 small balls. Dip in margarine; coat with combined sugar, nuts and cinnamon. Layer in lightly greased 6½-cup ring mold. Drizzle with remaining margarine; sprinkle with remaining sugar mixture. Let rise in warm place to top of mold, about 20 to 30 minutes. Place mold on cookie sheet. Bake at 425°, 15 to 20 minutes or until golden brown. Invert onto serving platter immediately.

Variation: Substitute 1 tablespoon orange rind for lemon.

Hoska

¾ cup milk   5½ cups flour
¾ cup sugar   3 eggs
½ teaspoon salt   ½ cup raisins
    Parkay margarine   ¼ cup chopped almonds
2 pkgs. active dry yeast   1 egg, beaten
    Water

Scald milk; stir in sugar, salt and ½ cup margarine. Cool to lukewarm. In large bowl, dissolve yeast in ½ cup warm water. Add milk mixture, 3 cups flour and 2 eggs; mix well. Stir in enough remaining flour to form a soft dough. On lightly floured surface, knead dough until smooth and elastic. Place in greased bowl; brush with melted margarine. Cover; let rise in warm place until double in volume, about 1 hour. Punch down dough. On lightly floured surface, knead in raisins and nuts. Divide dough into four equal pieces; reserve two pieces. Shape one piece into three 14-inch ropes. Place ropes on greased cookie sheet; braid. Brush with combined remaining egg and 1 tablespoon water. Shape two-thirds of second piece of dough into three 12-inch ropes; braid and place on top of first braid. Brush with egg mixture. Shape remaining one-third of dough into three 10-inch ropes; braid and place on top of second braid. Repeat procedure with remaining dough to form second loaf. Cover; let rise until double in volume, about 1 hour. Brush loaves with egg mixture. Garnish with whole blanched almonds, if desired. Bake at 375°, 25 minutes. Loaves will be well browned.

2 loaves

Hot Cross Buns

4 to 4½ cups flour	Parkay margarine
1 cup raisins	½ cup water
⅓ cup sugar	½ cup milk
2 pkgs. active dry yeast	2 eggs
1 teaspoon cinnamon	Quick Sugar Glaze
½ teaspoon salt	

In large mixing bowl, combine 1½ cups flour, raisins and remaining dry ingredients. Heat ½ cup margarine, water and milk over low heat until warm. Add to flour mixture; beat 2 minutes at medium speed of electric mixer. Add ½ cup flour and eggs; beat 2 minutes at high speed. Stir in enough additional flour to form a soft dough. On floured surface, knead dough until smooth and elastic, about 5 minutes. Cover; let rise until double in volume, about 20 minutes. Punch down dough; divide in half. Cut each half into twelve equal pieces. Shape each piece into smooth ball; place, 2 inches apart, on greased cookie sheet. Brush lightly with melted margarine. Cover; refrigerate 2 to 24 hours. Uncover; let stand 10 minutes. Cut shallow cross in top of each bun. Bake at 375°, 15 to 20 minutes. Cool slightly; glaze crosses with:

Quick Sugar Glaze

2 cups sifted confectioners' sugar	2 tablespoons milk
	1 teaspoon vanilla

Combine ingredients; mix well.

2 dozen

Pan Rolls Italiano

1 13¾-oz. pkg. hot roll mix	¾ cup (3 ozs.) Kraft grated
⅓ cup Parkay margarine, melted	parmesan cheese
½ teaspoon oregano leaves, crushed	

Prepare hot roll mix as directed on package. Cover; let rise in warm place until double in volume, about 1 hour. Shape dough into sixteen balls. Dip in combined margarine and oregano; roll in cheese. Place in well-greased 9-inch layer pan. Cover; let rise until double in volume, about 30 minutes. Bake at 400°, 15 to 20 minutes or until golden brown. Remove from pan immediately.

16 rolls

Rich Dinner Rolls

1 pkg. active dry yeast	Parkay margarine
⅓ cup warm water	2 teaspoons salt
⅔ cup milk	4½ to 5 cups flour
½ cup sugar	3 eggs, slightly beaten

Dissolve yeast in warm water. Heat milk, sugar, ½ cup margarine and salt over low heat until warm. In large mixing bowl, combine milk mixture and 1¼ cups flour; mix well. Add yeast and eggs; beat well. Stir in enough remaining flour to form a soft dough. On floured surface, knead dough until smooth and elastic. Place in greased bowl; brush with melted margarine. Cover; let rise in warm place until double in volume, about 1½ hours. Punch down dough. On lightly floured surface, shape as desired following directions below.

Fan-Tans

Divide dough into three equal pieces; shape each piece into a ball. Cover; let rest 10 minutes. Roll out each ball to 14 × 9-inch rectangle; brush with melted margarine. Cut rectangle lengthwise into six 1½-inch strips. Stack. Cut crosswise into eight ¾-inch pieces. Place in greased medium-size muffin pan, cut-side up. Cover; let rise until double in volume, about 1 hour. Bake at 375°, 15 minutes.

2 dozen

Butterhorns

Divide dough into three equal pieces; shape each piece into a ball. Cover; let rest 10 minutes. Roll out each ball to 12-inch circle. Brush with melted margarine. Cut circle into twelve wedges. Roll up each wedge, starting at wide end. Place rolls on greased cookie sheet, point-side down. Brush with melted margarine. Cover; let rise until double in volume, about 1 hour. Bake at 400°, 10 minutes.

3 dozen

Hot Cross Buns (page 13), Rich Dinner Rolls

Sweet Batter Rolls

leave cinnamon out use as dinner roll

3 to 3½ cups flour
⅓ cup sugar
2 pkgs. active dry yeast
1 teaspoon salt
½ cup Parkay margarine
½ cup milk
½ cup water

1 egg

* * *

¼ cup Parkay margarine, melted
¼ cup sugar
½ teaspoon cinnamon

In large mixing bowl, combine 1¾ cups flour, sugar, yeast and salt. Heat margarine, milk and water over low heat until warm. Add to flour mixture; beat 2 minutes at medium speed of electric mixer. Add ½ cup flour and egg; beat 2 minutes at high speed. Stir in enough additional flour to form a soft dough. Cover; let rise in warm place until double in volume, about 45 minutes. Punch dough down. On lightly floured surface, roll out dough to 20 × 10-inch rectangle.

Brush dough with 2 tablespoons margarine; sprinkle with combined sugar and cinnamon. Roll up, starting at long end; seal long end. Cut into twenty-four ¾-inch slices. Place in two greased 9-inch layer pans, cut-side up. Brush with remaining margarine. Cover; let rise until double in volume, about 30 minutes. Bake at 350°, 25 minutes.

2 dozen

Sally Lunn

4 cups flour
½ cup sugar
1 pkg. active dry yeast
½ teaspoon salt

½ cup Parkay margarine
½ cup milk
½ cup water
3 eggs

In large mixing bowl, combine 2 cups flour, sugar, yeast and salt. Heat margarine, milk and water over low heat until warm. Add to flour mixture; beat 2 minutes at medium speed of electric mixer. Blend in eggs; stir in remaining flour. Cover; let rise in warm place until double in volume, about 1 hour. Stir down dough; turn into well-greased and sugared 3-quart Kugelhupf mold or 10-inch tube pan. Cover; let rise until double in volume, about 1 hour. Bake at 400°, 25 to 30 minutes or until golden brown. Cool 5 minutes; remove from pan. Serve warm.

Raised Doughnuts

3¼ to 3¾ cups flour
⅓ cup sugar
2 pkgs. active dry yeast
½ teaspoon salt
1 cup milk

Parkay margarine
2 eggs
Oil
Doughnut Glaze

In large mixing bowl, combine 1½ cups flour, sugar, yeast and salt. Heat milk and ⅓ cup margarine over low heat until warm. Add to flour mixture; beat 1 minute at medium speed of electric mixer. Add eggs; beat 3 minutes at high speed. Stir in enough remaining flour to form a very soft dough. On lightly floured surface, knead dough ten times. Place in greased bowl; brush with melted margarine. Cover; let rise in warm place until double in volume, about 1 hour. Punch down dough; divide dough in half. Cover; let rest 10 minutes. On lightly floured surface, roll out each half to ½-inch thickness; cut with floured 3-inch doughnut cutter. Let rest, uncovered, 1 hour. Fry in deep hot oil, 375°, 2 to 4 minutes or until golden brown, turning once. Drain on absorbent paper. Dip in Doughnut Glaze while warm. Cool on rack on waxed paper.

Doughnut Glaze

1½ cups sifted confectioners'
    sugar

3 tablespoons water
1 teaspoon vanilla

Combine ingredients; mix well.

Approximately 2 dozen

When frying doughnuts, be sure to keep the oil at 375°. If the fat is too cool, the doughnuts will absorb the oil; if too hot, the dough will not be thoroughly cooked before the outside is browned.

Brioche

1 pkg. active dry yeast	3½ cups flour
¼ cup warm water	½ cup milk
½ cup Parkay margarine	½ teaspoon salt
⅓ cup sugar	1 tablespoon sugar
4 eggs	

Dissolve yeast in warm water. In large mixing bowl, cream margarine and sugar until light and fluffy. Separate 1 egg; reserve white. Add yeast, egg yolk, 3 eggs, 1 cup flour, milk and salt to creamed mixture; mix well. Stir in remaining flour; beat 5 to 8 minutes at medium speed of electric mixer. Cover; let rise in warm place until double in volume, about 2 hours. Stir down dough. Cover; refrigerate overnight. Stir down dough. On lightly floured surface, divide dough into four equal pieces; reserve one piece. Cut each remaining piece into eight pieces; shape into balls. Place in well-greased medium-size muffin pan. Cut reserved piece into 24 pieces; shape into small balls. Indent centers of each large ball; press one small ball into each indentation. Cover; let rise until double in volume, about 25 minutes. Combine reserved egg white and sugar; brush top of dough. Bake at 375°, 12 to 15 minutes or until golden brown.

2 dozen

Peach Crumb Coffee Cake

1¾ to 2¼ cups flour	2 eggs
½ cup granulated sugar	1 16-oz. can peach slices,
1 pkg. active dry yeast	well-drained, cut in half
½ teaspoon salt	½ cup packed brown sugar
⅔ cup Squeeze Parkay margarine	½ cup flour
¼ cup milk	1½ teaspoons nutmeg
¼ cup water	

In small bowl, combine 1 cup flour, granulated sugar, yeast and salt. Heat ⅓ cup margarine, milk and water over low heat until warm. Add to flour mixture; beat 2 minutes at medium speed of electric mixer. Add ½ cup flour and eggs; beat at high speed 2 minutes. Stir in enough remaining flour to form a stiff batter. Spread into well-greased 9-inch square pan. Arrange peaches evenly over batter. Sprinkle combined remaining margarine, brown sugar, flour and nutmeg over peaches. Cover; let rise in warm place until double in volume, about 25 minutes. Bake at 375°, 35 to 40 minutes or until wooden pick inserted in center comes out clean.

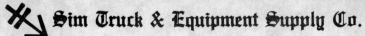

Sim Truck & Equipment Supply Co.

P. O. BOX 579   Sturgis, Michigan   49091

Area Code 616   Phone: 651-3235

DISTRIBUTOR FOR

Korody-Colyer Corporation

WORLD'S LARGEST MANUFACTURER OF
REPLACEMENT PARTS FOR
GENERAL MOTORS DIESEL ENGINES

Apple Rolls

3½ to 4½ cups flour
2 pkgs. active dry yeast
½ cup sugar
1 teaspoon salt
½ teaspoon cinnamon
1 cup milk
Parkay margarine

½ teaspoon almond extract
1 egg
1 20-oz. can apple pie
   filling
½ cup slivered almonds,
   toasted

In large mixing bowl, combine 2 cups flour, yeast, sugar, salt and cinnamon. Heat milk and ½ cup margarine over low heat until warm. Add to flour mixture with almond extract; beat 2 minutes at medium speed of electric mixer. Add egg and ½ cup flour; beat 2 minutes at high speed. Stir in enough remaining flour to form a soft dough. On floured surface, knead dough until smooth and elastic. Place in greased bowl; brush with melted margarine. Cover; let rise in warm place until double in volume, about 1 hour. Punch down dough; divide into eighteen equal pieces. Roll each piece into a rope 15-inches long. Shape each rope into a coil; tuck end under to seal. Place, 2 inches apart, on greased cookie sheet. Cover; let rise until double in volume, about 30 minutes. Indent centers; fill with pie filling. Sprinkle with nuts. Bake at 375°, 12 to 15 minutes or until golden brown.

1½ dozen

Honey Yeast Rolls

2 pkgs. active dry yeast
1 cup warm water
3½ to 4 cups flour
1 teaspoon salt

Parkay margarine, melted
1 egg, slightly beaten
2 tablespoons honey

Dissolve yeast in warm water. Combine 2 cups flour and salt. Add yeast, ¼ cup margarine, egg and honey; mix well. Stir in enough remaining flour to form a stiff dough. Place dough in greased bowl; brush with margarine. Cover; let rise in warm place until double in volume, about 20 minutes. Punch down dough; shape into 1-inch balls. Place three balls in each greased medium-size muffin cup. Cover; let rise until double in volume, about 20 minutes. Brush with margarine. Bake at 400°, 12 to 15 minutes or until lightly browned.

Approximately 2 dozen

Kolacky

4½ to 4¾ cups flour
½ cup sugar
2 pkgs. active dry yeast
1 teaspoon salt
¾ cup milk

Parkay margarine
3 eggs
½ teaspoon grated lemon rind
Cream Cheese Filling

In large mixing bowl, combine 1 cup flour, sugar, yeast and salt. Heat milk and ½ cup margarine over low heat until warm. Add to flour mixture; beat 3 minutes at medium speed of electric mixer. Add ½ cup flour, eggs and lemon rind; beat 2 minutes at high speed. Stir in enough remaining flour to form a soft dough. On lightly floured surface, knead dough until smooth and elastic, about 5 minutes. Place in greased bowl; brush with melted margarine. Cover; let rise in warm place until double in volume, about 1½ hours. Punch down dough; divide in half. Cover; let rest 10 minutes. Shape each half into twelve balls. Place, 3 inches apart, on greased cookie sheet; flatten to 3-inch circle. Cover; let rise until double in volume, about 45 minutes. Indent centers; fill with Cream Cheese Filling. Bake at 375°, 8 to 10 minutes or until golden brown. Remove from cookie sheet; sprinkle with sifted confectioners' sugar, if desired.

Cream Cheese Filling

1 8-oz. pkg. Philadelphia
    Brand cream cheese
¼ cup sugar

1 egg
¼ teaspoon grated lemon rind

Combine softened cream cheese and remaining ingredients, mixing until well blended.

2 dozen

Fast
Staff Of Life

When your busy schedule does
not allow the leisurely luxury of
yeast baking, the logical alter-
natives are quick breads—an
American innovation. Who
could resist the temptation of
Banana 'N Spice Nut Bread,
Almond Streusel Coffee Cake,
Golden Scones or Sunshine
Blueberry Loaf.

Almond Streusel Coffee Cake

¾ cup Parkay margarine
1½ cups granulated sugar
3 eggs
1½ teaspoons vanilla
½ teaspoon almond extract
2½ cups flour
2 teaspoons baking powder
1 teaspoon baking soda
1 teaspoon salt
1 cup plain yogurt or dairy
   sour cream

*   *   *

½ cup granulated sugar
½ cup packed brown sugar
¼ cup flour
4 teaspoons cinnamon
¼ cup Parkay margarine
1 cup old fashioned or quick
   oats, uncooked
¼ cup chopped almonds,
   toasted

Cream margarine and sugar until light and fluffy. Add eggs, one at a time, mixing well after each addition. Blend in vanilla and almond extract. Add combined dry ingredients alternately with yogurt, mixing well after each addition.

Combine sugars, flour and cinnamon; cut in margarine until mixture resembles coarse crumbs. Add oats and nuts; toss lightly. Pour half of batter into greased 13 × 9-inch baking pan; sprinkle with half of topping. Repeat layers. Bake at 350°, 45 to 50 minutes or until wooden pick inserted in center comes out clean.

Orange-Nut Loaf

¾ cup Squeeze Parkay margarine
1¼ cups sugar
3 eggs
2½ cups flour
2 teaspoons baking powder
1 teaspoon salt

½ cup milk
⅓ cup orange juice
½ cup chopped nuts
2 teaspoons grated
   orange rind

Combine margarine and sugar. Blend in eggs. Add combined dry ingredients alternately with milk and orange juice, mixing just until moistened. Stir in nuts and orange rind. Pour into greased and floured 9 × 5-inch loaf pan. Bake at 350°, 1 hour and 20 minutes or until wooden pick inserted in center comes out clean. Cool 5 minutes; remove from pan.

A Few Reminders

- All ingredients should be at room temperature, except when a recipe indicates that the margarine is to be "cut in." Then the margarine should be at refrigerator temperature.

- When eggs are added "one at a time," each egg should be thoroughly blended with the creamed margarine and sugar before the next egg is added.

- For biscuit-type doughs, dry ingredients are mixed "just until moistened." The dough will be slightly lumpy, not smooth.

- Roll out dough with a light pressure. Avoid excessive re-rolling.

- To remove breads, rolls or muffins from pans, gently run a spatula around sides; invert on cooling rack and turn upright.

Apple Spice Coffee Cake

½ cup Parkay margarine
1 cup granulated sugar
¾ cup packed brown sugar
2 eggs
1 teaspoon vanilla
3 cups flour
1 tablespoon baking powder
1 teaspoon salt
1 teaspoon ground allspice
1 teaspoon ground cloves
1 cup milk
3 cups peeled apple slices
1 teaspoon cinnamon

Cream margarine, ¾ cup granulated sugar and brown sugar until light and fluffy. Blend in eggs and vanilla. Add combined flour, baking powder, salt, allspice and cloves alternately with milk; mix well after each addition. Pour into greased 13 × 9-inch baking pan. Arrange apples on batter; sprinkle with combined ¼ cup granulated sugar and cinnamon. Bake at 375°, 40 to 45 minutes or until wooden pick inserted in center comes out clean.

Breakfast Orange Crumb Cake

½ cup Parkay margarine
¾ cup granulated sugar
1 egg
1 tablespoon grated orange
   rind
2 cups flour
2 teaspoons baking powder
½ teaspoon salt
½ cup orange juice

⅓ cup milk

       *   *   *

½ cup packed brown sugar
2 tablespoons flour
1 teaspoon cinnamon
2 tablespoons Parkay
   margarine
½ cup chopped nuts

Cream margarine and granulated sugar until light and fluffy. Blend in egg and orange rind. Add combined flour, baking powder and salt alternately with orange juice and milk, mixing well after each addition. Pour into greased 9-inch square pan.

Combine brown sugar, flour and cinnamon; cut in margarine until mixture resembles coarse crumbs. Stir in nuts; sprinkle over batter. Bake at 375°, 35 to 40 minutes or until wooden pick inserted in center comes out clean.

Treasure Chest Loaves

2 cups flour
1 tablespoon sugar
1½ teaspoons baking powder
1 teaspoon salt
¼ cup Parkay margarine
1½ cups (6 ozs.) shredded Kraft
   natural Swiss cheese

2 teaspoons poppy seed
1 egg, slightly beaten
1 cup milk
2 teaspoons Kraft pure
   prepared mustard

Combine dry ingredients; cut in margarine until mixture resembles coarse crumbs. Stir in cheese and poppy seed. Add combined egg, milk and mustard, mixing just until moistened. Grease and flour 9 × 5-inch loaf pan; divide into four sections with two 7-inch L-shaped pieces of greased aluminum foil. Spoon one fourth batter into each section of loaf pan. Bake at 350°, 1 hour and 15 minutes. Remove from pan immediately; remove aluminum foil.

4 loaves

Orange Coffee Cake

½ cup Parkay margarine
1¼ cups sugar
2 eggs
2¼ cups flour
1 tablespoon baking powder
1 teaspoon salt
¾ cup milk
¼ cup water

1 8-oz. pkg. Philadelphia
  Brand cream cheese, cubed
½ cup chopped nuts
1 tablespoon grated orange
  rind
*   *   *
¼ cup sugar
2 teaspoons grated orange
  rind

Cream margarine and sugar until light and fluffy. Blend in eggs. Add combined dry ingredients alternately with milk and water, mixing well after each addition. Fold in cream cheese, nuts and orange rind. Pour into greased and floured 13 × 9-inch baking pan.

Sprinkle combined sugar and orange rind over batter; press lightly into batter. Bake at 375°, 35 to 40 minutes or until wooden pick inserted in center comes out clean.

Variation: Substitute 9 × 5-inch loaf pan for baking pan. Decrease topping to 2 tablespoons sugar and 1 teaspoon grated orange rind. Bake at 375°, 1 hour and 15 to 20 minutes or until wooden pick inserted in center comes out clean.

Bacon 'N Onion Cornbread

¼ cup Parkay margarine
2 eggs
1½ cups cornmeal
½ cup flour
1 tablespoon sugar
2 teaspoons baking powder

1½ teaspoons salt
½ teaspoon baking soda
1½ cups buttermilk
8 crisply cooked bacon
  slices, crumbled
¼ cup chopped onion

Cream margarine; blend in eggs. Add combined dry ingredients alternately with buttermilk; mix well after each addition. Stir in half of bacon and onion. Pour into greased and floured 8-inch square pan. Sprinkle with remaining bacon and onion. Bake at 350°, 30 to 35 minutes.

Zucchini Bread

¾ cup Parkay margarine
1 cup sugar
4 eggs
2 teaspoons vanilla
1½ cups shredded zucchini
3 cups flour

2 teaspoons baking powder
1½ teaspoons pumpkin pie spice
1 teaspoon baking soda
1 teaspoon salt
1 cup chopped nuts

Cream margarine and sugar until light and fluffy. Blend in eggs and vanilla. Stir in zucchini. Add combined dry ingredients; mix well. Stir in nuts. Pour into greased and floured 9 × 5-inch loaf pan. Bake at 350°, 1 hour and 10 minutes or until wooden pick inserted in center comes out clean. Cool 5 minutes; remove from pan.

Onion Flat Bread

½ cup chopped onion
½ cup Squeeze Parkay margarine
2 cups flour
1 tablespoon baking powder
½ teaspoon salt

½ teaspoon oregano leaves, crushed
1 egg, slightly beaten
⅓ cup milk

Sauté onion in margarine. Combine dry ingredients. Add combined onion, egg and milk, mixing just until moistened. Spread into 9-inch pie plate. Bake at 425°, 25 minutes. Serve warm.

Banana 'N Spice Nut Bread

½ cup Parkay margarine
¾ cup sugar
2 eggs
1 teaspoon vanilla
2 cups flour
1½ teaspoons baking powder
½ teaspoon baking soda

½ teaspoon salt
½ teaspoon cinnamon
¼ teaspoon ground allspice
¼ teaspoon ground cloves
1 cup mashed bananas
½ cup chopped nuts

Cream margarine and sugar until light and fluffy. Blend in eggs and vanilla. Add combined dry ingredients alternately with bananas, mixing well after each addition. Stir in nuts. Pour into greased and floured 9 × 5-inch loaf pan. Bake at 350°, 55 to 60 minutes or until wooden pick inserted in center comes out clean. Cool 5 minutes; remove from pan.

Sunshine Blueberry Loaf

½ cup Squeeze Parkay margarine
1 cup sugar
3 eggs
2 teaspoons grated lemon rind
3 cups flour
1 tablespoon baking powder
1 teaspoon salt

¼ teaspoon baking soda
1¼ cups Kraft pure 100%
    unsweetened pasteurized
    orange juice
1 cup fresh blueberries
½ cup chopped nuts

Combine margarine and sugar. Blend in eggs and lemon rind. Add combined dry ingredients alternately with orange juice, mixing well after each addition. Fold in blueberries and nuts. Pour into greased and floured 9 × 5-inch loaf pan. Bake at 350°, 1 hour and 15 minutes or until wooden pick inserted in center comes out clean. Cool 5 minutes; remove from pan.

Country Caraway Bread

1 cup all-purpose flour
1 cup whole-wheat flour
½ cup sugar
2 teaspoons caraway seed
1½ teaspoons baking powder
½ teaspoon baking soda

½ teaspoon salt
2 eggs, slightly beaten
½ cup Squeeze Parkay
    margarine
½ cup milk

Combine dry ingredients. Add combined eggs, margarine and milk, mixing just until moistened. Pour into greased and floured 9 × 5-inch loaf pan. Bake at 350°, 50 to 60 minutes or until wooden pick inserted in center comes out clean. Cool 5 minutes; remove from pan.

Homemade and easy, quick breads are perfect gifts. Keep a loaf or two in the freezer as ready offerings - for new neighbors, hostess "thank yous" or to welcome home vacationing friends.

Cranberry Orange Bread

3 cups flour
¾ cup sugar
1 tablespoon baking powder
1 teaspoon salt
½ teaspoon baking soda
2 eggs, slightly beaten
1 cup Kraft pure 100%
    unsweetened pasteurized
    orange juice
½ cup Squeeze Parkay
    margarine
1¼ cups cranberries, coarsely
    chopped
½ cup chopped nuts

Combine dry ingredients. Add combined eggs, orange juice and margarine, mixing just until moistened. Stir in cranberries and nuts. Pour into greased and floured 9 × 5-inch loaf pan. Bake at 350°, 1 hour and 15 minutes or until wooden pick inserted in center comes out clean. Cool 5 minutes; remove from pan.

Deliciously colorful, a lovely loaf for entertaining, festive family meals or afternoon teas.

Hearty Cornbread

1 cup cornmeal
1 cup flour
1 tablespoon baking powder
1 teaspoon salt
2 cups (8 ozs.) shredded
    Casino brand natural
    monterey jack cheese
1 egg, slightly beaten
1 cup milk
¼ cup Squeeze Parkay
    margarine
1 green pepper, cut into
    rings

Combine dry ingredients; stir in 1 cup cheese. Add combined egg, milk and margarine, mixing just until moistened. Pour into greased 9-inch layer pan. Cover with remaining cheese; top with green pepper. Bake at 425°, 20 minutes.

A super, savory bread for chili dinners or for "brown bagging" with a thermos of soup.

Honey Corn Muffins

1 cup flour
1 cup cornmeal
4 teaspoons baking powder
½ teaspoon salt
1 12-oz. can mexicorn or whole
  kernel corn, drained

1 egg, slightly beaten
1 cup milk
⅓ cup Parkay margarine,
  melted
⅓ cup honey

Combine dry ingredients; stir in corn. Add combined remaining ingredients, mixing just until moistened. Spoon into greased medium-size muffin pan, filling each cup ⅔ full. Bake at 400°, 20 to 25 minutes or until lightly browned.

1½ dozen

Break the lunch box routine with a hearty mexicorn muffin.

Blueberry Muffins

2 cups flour
⅓ cup sugar
2 teaspoons baking powder
½ teaspoon salt
1 egg, slightly beaten

¾ cup milk
½ cup Parkay margarine,
  melted
1 cup fresh blueberries

Combine dry ingredients. Add combined egg, milk and margarine, mixing just until moistened. Fold in blueberries. Spoon into greased and floured medium-size muffin pan, filling each cup ⅔ full. Bake at 425°, 20 to 25 minutes or until golden brown.

1 dozen

Variations: Substitute for fresh blueberries 1 cup:

- Well-drained, thawed frozen blueberries or cranberries
- Well-drained pitted dark sweet cherries
- Fresh cranberries

Lemon Muffins

2 cups flour
⅓ cup sugar
1 tablespoon grated lemon rind
2 teaspoons baking powder
½ teaspoon salt

1 egg, slightly beaten
½ cup Squeeze Parkay
   margarine
½ cup milk
¼ cup lemon juice

Combine dry ingredients. Add combined egg, margarine, milk and lemon juice; mix just until moistened. Spoon into greased and floured medium-size muffin pan, filling each cup ⅔ full. Bake at 425°, 20 to 25 minutes or until lightly brown.

1 dozen

Jubilee Muffins

½ cup Parkay margarine
½ cup packed brown sugar
1 10-oz. jar Kraft apricot
   or peach preserves
½ cup milk
2 eggs

2¾ cups flour
2 teaspoons baking powder
1 teaspoon salt
½ teaspoon baking soda
½ cup chopped nuts

Cream margarine and sugar until light and fluffy. Blend in preserves, milk and eggs. Add combined dry ingredients, mixing just until moistened. Stir in nuts. Spoon into greased and floured medium-size muffin pan, filling each cup ⅔ full. Bake at 350°, 25 to 30 minutes or until lightly browned.

1½ dozen

Pecan Pull-Apart

2 8-oz. cans Pillsbury
   refrigerated quick Crescent
   dinner rolls
½ cup Parkay margarine, melted

1 cup sugar
⅓ cup finely chopped pecans
1¼ teaspoons cinnamon

Separate dough into rectangles. Cut each rectangle in half lengthwise. Roll dough strips into ropes 12 inches long. Dip each rope in margarine; roll in combined sugar, nuts and cinnamon. Line 14-inch pizza pan with aluminum foil; grease well. Starting at center of pan, loosely arrange ropes in spiral fashion. Bake at 375°, 20 to 25 minutes or until golden brown.

Golden Scones

⅔ cup Parkay margarine,
  melted
¼ cup sugar
⅓ cup milk
1 egg
1½ cups old fashioned or
  quick oats, uncooked

1½ cups flour
1 tablespoon baking powder
½ teaspoon salt
½ cup golden raisins
½ cup chopped walnuts

Combine margarine and sugar. Blend in milk and egg. Add combined remaining ingredients, mixing just until moistened. On lightly floured surface, roll out dough to 12 × 9-inch rectangle. Cut into twelve 3-inch squares; cut each square in half diagonally. Place on ungreased cookie sheet. Bake at 425°, 10 to 12 minutes or until lightly browned. Serve with honey and additional margarine, if desired.

2 dozen

An Americanized version of an English tradition, serve these versatile scones for breakfast, brunch or lunch with honey or marmalade.

Hearty Cheddar Biscuits

2 cups flour
1 tablespoon baking powder
1 teaspoon salt
¼ cup Parkay margarine
1½ cups (6 ozs.) shredded Kraft
  sharp natural cheddar
  cheese

½ cup chopped onion
2 tablespoons chopped
  pimiento
¾ cup milk

Combine dry ingredients; cut in margarine until mixture resembles coarse crumbs. Stir in cheese, onion and pimiento. Add milk, mixing just until moistened. On lightly floured surface, knead dough ten times. Roll out dough to ½-inch thickness; cut with floured 2½ to 3-inch cutter. Place on greased cookie sheet. Bake at 450°, 12 minutes or until golden brown.

Approximately 2 dozen

Boston Bran Muffins

1½ cups flour
1 cup bran cereal
1 teaspoon salt
1 teaspoon baking powder
½ teaspoon baking soda

1 egg, slightly beaten
1 cup milk
⅓ cup Parkay margarine,
 melted
¼ cup dark molasses

Combine dry ingredients. Add combined egg, milk, margarine and molasses, mixing just until moistened. Spoon into greased medium-size muffin pan, filling each cup ⅔ full. Bake at 400°, 25 minutes.

8 muffins

Sesame Seed Twists

1 cup flour
1½ teaspoons baking powder
¼ teaspoon salt
 Parkay margarine

⅓ cup milk
2 tablespoons toasted sesame
 seed or poppy seed

Combine flour, baking powder and salt; cut in ¼ cup margarine until mixture resembles coarse crumbs. Add milk, mixing just until moistened. On lightly floured surface, knead dough about 15 times. Roll out dough to 12 × 6-inch rectangle. Brush with 2 tablespoons melted margarine. Sprinkle with seed; press lightly into dough. Cut dough into twenty-four 6 × ½-inch strips. Place on ungreased cookie sheet; twist strips. Bake at 450°, 10 to 12 minutes or until lightly browned.

2 dozen

Parmesan Pillows

2 cups all-purpose biscuit mix
⅓ cup Parkay margarine, melted

1 cup (4 ozs.) Kraft grated
 parmesan cheese

Prepare biscuit mix as directed on package for rolled biscuits. On lightly floured surface, knead dough ten times. Roll out dough to 10 × 6-inch rectangle. Cut into 2-inch squares; cut each square in half diagonally. Dip in margarine; coat with cheese. Place on greased cookie sheet. Bake at 450°, 6 to 8 minutes or until lightly browned. Serve warm.

Approximately 2½ dozen

Boston Bran Muffins, Sesame Seed Twists, Parmesan Pillows

Savory Drop Biscuits

1¾ cups flour
1 tablespoon baking powder
½ teaspoon salt
½ teaspoon sage
½ teaspoon caraway seed

¼ teaspoon dry mustard
1 cup milk
¼ cup Squeeze Parkay
   margarine

Combine dry ingredients. Add combined milk and margarine, mixing just until moistened. Drop slightly rounded tablespoonfuls of batter onto greased cookie sheet. Bake at 450°, 10 to 12 minutes or until lightly browned.

1 dozen

Tiny Temptations

The word cookie comes from a Dutch word "koekie" meaning small cake. These cookies provide home-baked treats that are sure to make your kitchen the most popular room in the house.

Cookie Baking Tips

- Use shiny cookie sheets for evenly baked cookies.

- Cookie sheets should be at least 2 inches narrower and shorter than the oven to allow heat to circulate freely for even browning.

- For molded, pressed, refrigerated or rolled cookies, use a small amount of dough at one time. Keep remaining dough chilled.

- Make cookies of uniform size to insure even baking.

- Check at minimum baking time — a minute can make a difference.

- Allow hot cookie sheets to cool before reusing.

- Baked cookies should be cooled in a single layer on cooling racks.

- Cookie dough or baked cookies can be frozen and stored up to 6 months.

Pecan-Fruit Fancies

1 cup Squeeze Parkay margarine	2 cups flour
½ cup granulated sugar	1 teaspoon baking soda
½ cup packed brown sugar	½ teaspoon salt
2 eggs	1 cup mixed diced candied
1 teaspoon vanilla	fruit
2½ cups old fashioned or quick oats, uncooked	½ cup chopped pecans

Combine margarine and sugars. Blend in eggs and vanilla. Add combined dry ingredients; mix well. Stir in candied fruit and nuts. Drop rounded teaspoonfuls of dough onto greased cookie sheet. Bake at 350°, 12 to 15 minutes or until edges are golden brown.

Approximately 4½ dozen

Types of Cookies

Cookies are classified by the way they are formed:

- Bar Cookies - are quickly mixed, spread in a pan and baked. When cool, cut into squares or bars.

- Drop Cookies - have a soft dough which can be dropped by a spoon onto a cookie sheet.

- Molded Cookies - are made with a dough that is chilled to make handling easier. The chilled dough is formed into a variety of shapes — crescents, balls and logs.

- Pressed Cookies - have a stiff dough which is forced through a cookie press into decorative shapes — stars, trees and rosettes.

- Refrigerated Cookies - are usually round. The dough is formed into a roll and chilled. When ready to bake, the rolls are sliced using a very sharp knife.

- Rolled Cookies - have a stiff dough which is usually chilled. The dough is rolled to a specific thickness and cut with floured cookie cutters.

Chewy Orange Delights

¾ cup Parkay margarine	3 cups flour
1 cup packed brown sugar	½ teaspoon baking powder
¼ cup granulated sugar	½ teaspoon baking soda
⅓ cup dairy sour cream	½ teaspoon salt
2 eggs	1⅓ cups shredded coconut
1½ teaspoons vanilla	½ cup chopped walnuts
1 teaspoon grated orange rind	

Cream margarine and sugars until light and fluffy. Blend in sour cream, eggs, vanilla and orange rind. Add combined dry ingredients; mix well. Stir in coconut and nuts. Drop rounded teaspoonfuls of dough onto ungreased cookie sheet. Bake at 400°, 10 to 12 minutes or until golden brown.

Approximately 6½ dozen

Flavor-Favorite Bars

1 cup Squeeze Parkay
  margarine
1 cup sugar
1 egg
1 teaspoon vanilla

2 cups flour
½ cup semi-sweet chocolate
  pieces
½ cup finely chopped peanuts
  or pecans

Combine margarine and sugar. Blend in egg and vanilla. Add flour; mix well. Spread into ungreased 15½×10½-inch jelly roll pan. Sprinkle with chocolate pieces and nuts; press lightly into batter. Bake at 300°, 35 to 40 minutes or until edges are very lightly browned. Cool; cut into bars.

Variations: Substitute 1 cup toasted shredded coconut for chocolate pieces and nuts.

Substitute 1 cup mixed diced candied fruit for chocolate pieces and nuts. Combine 1 cup sifted confectioners' sugar and 2 tablespoons milk; drizzle over bars immediately after baking.

Substitute ¾ cup chopped pitted dates and ½ cup chopped walnuts for chocolate pieces and nuts. Combine 1 cup sifted confectioners' sugar and 2 tablespoons milk; drizzle over bars immediately after baking.

Cherry Charms

1 cup Parkay margarine
1 cup sugar
2 tablespoons milk
1 teaspoon vanilla
3 cups flour
½ teaspoon salt

½ cup chopped green candied
  cherries
½ cup chopped red candied
  cherries
1 cup finely chopped pecans

Cream margarine and sugar until light and fluffy. Blend in milk and vanilla. Add combined flour, salt and cherries; mix well. Shape dough into two 12-inch rolls; roll in nuts. Wrap securely; chill several hours or overnight. Cut rolls into ¼-inch slices; place on ungreased cookie sheet. Bake at 375°, 10 to 12 minutes or until edges are lightly browned.

Approximately 7 dozen

Date Hermits

½ cup Parkay margarine
⅔ cup packed brown sugar
1 egg
½ teaspoon vanilla
2 cups flour
2 teaspoons baking powder

1 teaspoon cinnamon
½ teaspoon salt
½ teaspoon nutmeg
¼ teaspoon ground cloves
¼ cup milk
1 cup chopped pitted dates

Cream margarine and sugar until light and fluffy. Blend in egg and vanilla. Add combined dry ingredients alternately with milk, mixing well after each addition. Stir in dates. Drop rounded teaspoonfuls of dough onto ungreased cookie sheet. Bake at 350°, 12 to 15 minutes or until golden brown.

Approximately 3 dozen

Cookie Ornaments

1 cup Parkay margarine
1 cup sugar
2 eggs
3 cups flour

½ teaspoon baking soda
½ teaspoon baking powder
Glaze
Colored yarn

Cream margarine and sugar until light and fluffy. Blend in eggs. Add combined dry ingredients; mix well. Chill one hour. Divide dough into four portions. On lightly floured surface, roll out dough ⅛-inch thick; cut three portions with 4-inch round cookie cutter. With end of large straw, cut small hole near edge of each cookie. Cut remaining dough with assorted 1½-inch cookie cutters. Place on ungreased cookie sheet. Bake at 375°, 6 to 8 minutes or until edges are lightly browned. Cool. Spread cookies with Glaze; decorate as desired. Secure small cookies to top of large ones using additional Glaze. Let stand until Glaze is set; tie 4 to 6-inch pieces of yarn through holes.

Glaze

2 cups sifted confectioners' sugar

¼ cup milk
Food coloring

Combine sugar and milk; mix well. Tint as desired with food coloring.

Approximately 1½ dozen

Thick And Chewy Chocolate Bars

1 cup Parkay margarine
½ cup packed brown sugar
½ cup granulated sugar
2 eggs
1 teaspoon vanilla
1¼ cups flour

1 teaspoon baking soda
1½ cups old fashioned or quick
    oats, uncooked
1 12-oz. pkg. semi-sweet
    chocolate pieces
1 cup chopped nuts

Cream margarine and sugars until light and fluffy. Blend in eggs and vanilla. Add combined flour and baking soda; mix well. Stir in oats, chocolate pieces and nuts. Spread into well-greased 13 × 9-inch baking pan. Bake at 375°, 25 to 30 minutes or until golden brown. Cool; cut into bars.

Variation: Prepare cookie dough as directed. Drop rounded teaspoonfuls of dough onto ungreased cookie sheet. Bake at 375°, 10 to 12 minutes.

Approximately 5 dozen.

Ambrosia Drops

½ cup Parkay margarine
½ cup granulated sugar
½ cup packed brown sugar
2 eggs
1 tablespoon grated orange
    rind
1 teaspoon vanilla

2½ cups flour
½ teaspoon baking soda
½ teaspoon salt
1 cup chopped pecans
2 cups flaked coconut
Maraschino cherry halves

Cream margarine and sugars until light and fluffy. Blend in eggs, orange rind and vanilla. Add combined dry ingredients; mix well. Stir in nuts. Chill. Shape rounded teaspoonfuls of dough into balls; roll in coconut. Place on ungreased cookie sheet; top each ball with cherry half. Bake at 375°, 12 to 15 minutes or until golden brown.

Approximately 4 dozen

Honey Delights

½ cup Parkay margarine
¼ cup sugar
½ cup honey
1 egg
1 teaspoon vanilla
1 cup flour

½ teaspoon salt
½ teaspoon cinnamon
¼ teaspoon baking soda
1 cup old fashioned or quick
  oats, uncooked
1 cup raisins

Cream margarine and sugar until light and fluffy. Blend in honey, egg and vanilla. Add combined flour, salt, cinnamon and baking soda; mix well. Stir in oats and raisins. Drop rounded teaspoonfuls of dough onto ungreased cookie sheet. Bake at 375°, 10 to 12 minutes or until golden brown. Remove from cookie sheet immediately.

Approximately 3 dozen

Sour Cream Raisin Drops

½ cup Parkay margarine
¾ cup sugar
1 egg
½ teaspoon vanilla
1½ cups flour

½ teaspoon baking soda
¼ teaspoon salt
½ cup dairy sour cream
1 cup raisins
Orange Frosting

Cream margarine and sugar until light and fluffy. Blend in egg and vanilla. Add combined dry ingredients alternately with sour cream, mixing well after each addition. Add raisins. Drop rounded teaspoonfuls of dough onto ungreased cookie sheet. Bake at 375°, 8 to 10 minutes or until set. Cool; frost with Orange Frosting. Garnish with additional raisins, if desired.

Orange Frosting

¼ cup Parkay margarine
1 teaspoon grated orange rind

2 cups sifted confectioners'
  sugar
4 teaspoons milk

Cream margarine; blend in orange rind. Add sugar alternately with milk, beating until light and fluffy.

Approximately 5 dozen

Swiss Chocolate Squares

1 cup water	2 eggs
½ cup Parkay margarine	½ cup dairy sour cream
1½ 1-oz. squares unsweetened	1 teaspoon baking soda
chocolate	½ teaspoon salt
2 cups flour	Chocolate Frosting
2 cups sugar	½ cup chopped nuts

Combine water, margarine and chocolate in saucepan; bring to boil. Remove from heat. Stir in combined flour and sugar. Add eggs, sour cream, baking soda and salt; mix well. Pour into greased and floured 15½×10½-inch jelly roll pan. Bake at 375°, 20 to 25 minutes or until wooden pick inserted in center comes out clean. Frost cake while warm with Chocolate Frosting; sprinkle with nuts. Cool; cut into squares.

Chocolate Frosting

½ cup Parkay margarine	4½ cups sifted confectioners'
6 tablespoons milk	sugar
1½ 1-oz. squares unsweetened	1 teaspoon vanilla
chocolate	

Combine margarine, milk and chocolate in saucepan; bring to boil. Remove from heat. Add sugar; beat until smooth. Stir in vanilla.

Lemon Praline Cookies

¾ cup Parkay margarine	2 teaspoons grated lemon rind
¾ cup packed brown sugar	2¼ cups flour
¾ cup granulated sugar	1½ teaspoons baking powder
2 eggs	1 cup chopped pecans
1 tablespoon lemon juice	

Cream margarine and sugars until light and fluffy. Blend in eggs, lemon juice and lemon rind. Add combined dry ingredients; mix well. Stir in nuts. Chill. Drop rounded teaspoonfuls of dough onto greased cookie sheet. Bake at 375°, 10 to 12 minutes or until golden brown.

Approximately 6 dozen

Bristol Cinnamon Tea Cakes

1¼ cups sugar
½ cup Squeeze Parkay
  margarine
¾ cup buttermilk
1 egg
1 teaspoon vanilla

2¼ cups flour
1 teaspoon baking powder
½ teaspoon salt
¼ teaspoon baking soda
¼ teaspoon nutmeg
1 teaspoon cinnamon

Combine 1 cup sugar and margarine. Blend in buttermilk, egg and vanilla. Add flour, baking powder, salt, baking soda and nutmeg; mix until well blended. Drop rounded teaspoonfuls of dough, 2 inches apart, onto ungreased cookie sheet. Sprinkle cookies with combined remaining sugar and cinnamon. Bake at 400°, 10 to 12 minutes or until edges are golden brown. Remove from cookie sheet immediately.

Approximately 3½ dozen

Chewy Molasses Bars

½ cup Parkay margarine
½ cup sugar
½ cup light molasses
2 eggs
1½ cups flour
2 teaspoons baking powder

1 teaspoon cinnamon
½ teaspoon salt
¼ teaspoon ginger
1 cup raisins
Orange Frosting

Cream margarine and sugar until light and fluffy. Blend in molasses and eggs. Add combined dry ingredients; mix well. Stir in raisins. Pour into greased and floured 13×9-inch baking pan. Bake at 350°, 25 minutes or until wooden pick inserted in center comes out clean. Cool; frost with Orange Frosting. Cut into bars.

Orange Frosting

⅓ cup Parkay margarine
1 teaspoon grated orange rind

3 cups sifted confectioners'
  sugar
3 tablespoons orange juice

Cream margarine; blend in orange rind. Add sugar alternately with orange juice, beating until light and fluffy.

Viennese Cookies

1 cup Parkay margarine	½ cup ground almonds
1 cup granulated sugar	½ teaspoon salt
1 egg	Confectioners' sugar
1 teaspoon almond extract	Kraft strawberry, grape or
1 teaspoon grated lemon rind	peach preserves
2 cups flour	

Cream margarine and granulated sugar until light and fluffy. Blend in egg, almond extract and lemon rind. Add flour, nuts and salt; mix well. Chill. On lightly floured surface, roll out dough to ⅛-inch thickness; cut with 2-inch round cookie cutter. Cut small hole in center of half of cookies. Place on ungreased cookie sheet. Bake at 375°, 5 to 7 minutes or until edges are lightly browned. Cool. Sprinkle cookies with hole in center with confectioners' sugar. Spread remaining cookies with approximately ½ teaspoon preserves; top with sugar-covered cookies.

Approximately 5 dozen

Variations: Substitute ½ cup finely chopped almonds for ground almonds.

Substitute Kraft orange marmalade for preserves.

Choco-Peanut Butter Cookies

Fair

½ cup Parkay margarine	1 teaspoon vanilla
1 cup packed brown sugar	1½ cups flour
½ cup peanut butter	½ teaspoon baking soda
1 1-oz. square unsweetened	½ teaspoon salt
chocolate, melted	Granulated sugar
1 egg	

Cream margarine and brown sugar until light and fluffy. Blend in peanut butter, chocolate, egg and vanilla. Add combined flour, baking soda and salt; mix well. Shape rounded teaspoonfuls of dough into balls; roll in granulated sugar. Place on lightly greased cookie sheet; flatten slightly. Bake at 350°, 12 to 15 minutes or until lightly browned.

Approximately 4 dozen

Spritz

1 cup Parkay margarine	2½ cups flour
⅔ cup sugar	½ teaspoon baking powder
1 egg	Dash of salt
¼ teaspoon almond extract	

Cream margarine and sugar until light and fluffy. Blend in egg and almond extract. Add combined dry ingredients; mix well. Force dough through cookie press onto greased cookie sheet. Bake at 400°, 6 to 8 minutes or until edges are very lightly browned.

Approximately 6 dozen

Variation: Substitute ¼ teaspoon vanilla for almond extract.

Pumpkin Spice Cookies

1 cup Parkay margarine	2½ cups flour
1½ cups sugar	¾ teaspoon pumpkin pie spice
1 egg	Vanilla Glaze

Cream margarine and sugar until light and fluffy. Blend in egg. Add combined flour and spice; mix well. Chill. On lightly floured surface, roll out dough to ⅛-inch thickness; cut with 3-inch round cookie cutter. Place on greased cookie sheet. Bake at 400°, 6 to 8 minutes or until edges are very lightly browned. Cool; glaze with:

Vanilla Glaze

3 cups sifted confectioners' sugar	½ teaspoon vanilla
¼ cup milk	Dash of salt

Combine sugar, milk, vanilla, and salt; mix well. Tint with food coloring, if desired.

Approximately 5 dozen

Austrian Fruit 'N Cheese Bars

2¾ cups flour
1 teaspoon baking powder
½ teaspoon salt
¾ cup Parkay margarine
2 cups (8 ozs.) shredded Kraft
    sharp natural cheddar cheese

2 eggs
½ cup Kraft peach preserves
½ cup Kraft strawberry
    preserves

Combine dry ingredients; cut in margarine until mixture resembles coarse crumbs. Stir in cheese. Blend in eggs. Chill one quarter of dough. Press remaining dough onto bottom and sides of 15½×10½-inch jelly roll pan. Spread half of dough with peach preserves; spread remaining half with strawberry preserves. On lightly floured surface, roll out chilled dough; cut into ½-inch strips. Place strips diagonally across preserves to form lattice; press edges to seal. Bake at 350°, 35 minutes or until lightly brown. Cool; cut into bars.

A jelly roll pan is a cookie sheet with 1-inch sides.

Date Swirl Cookies

1 8-oz. pkg. chopped dates
¼ cup sugar
¼ cup water
    *   *   *
½ cup Parkay margarine
½ cup granulated sugar

½ cup packed brown sugar
1 egg
2 cups flour
½ teaspoon baking soda
½ teaspoon cinnamon
½ teaspoon salt

Combine dates, sugar and water in saucepan. Cook over low heat until dates are softened, stirring occasionally. Cool.
  Cream margarine and sugars until light and fluffy. Blend in egg. Add combined dry ingredients; mix well. On lightly floured surface, roll out dough to 10×14-inch rectangle. Spread date mixture over dough; roll up from long end. Wrap securely; chill. Cut roll into ¼-inch slices; place on ungreased cookie sheet. Bake at 350°, 10 to 12 minutes or until lightly browned.

Approximately 3 dozen

Scandinavian Almond Crescents

1 cup Parkay margarine	2¼ cups flour
Sifted confectioners' sugar	½ cup finely chopped almonds,
1½ teaspoons almond extract	toasted

Cream margarine and ¼ cup sugar until light and fluffy. Blend in almond extract. Add flour; mix well. Stir in nuts. Shape level teaspoonfuls of dough into crescents; place on ungreased cookie sheet. Bake at 325°, 25 to 30 minutes or until lightly browned. Remove from cookie sheet immediately. Cool 5 minutes; sprinkle lightly with additional sugar.

Approximately 5 dozen

Variation: Shape dough into balls and bake as directed.

Shaped into balls or crescents, these Scandinavian cookies are traditional for special celebrations.

Peanut Butter Sandwich Cookies

½ cup Parkay margarine	½ teaspoon vanilla
½ cup granulated sugar	1¼ cups flour
½ cup packed brown sugar	½ teaspoon baking soda
½ cup peanut butter	¼ teaspoon salt
1 egg	Kraft marshmallows

Cream margarine and sugars until light and fluffy. Blend in peanut butter, egg and vanilla. Add combined dry ingredients; mix well. Shape rounded teaspoonfuls of dough into balls. Place on ungreased cookie sheet; flatten balls with bottom of glass. Bake at 350°, 8 to 10 minutes or until lightly browned. Cool. For each sandwich cookie, top one cookie with hot toasted marshmallow and second cookie; press together slightly.

2 dozen

"Tote" these cookies to outdoor gatherings and toast the marshmallows over the open fire.

Oatmeal Crispies

1 cup Parkay margarine	1 teaspoon cream of tartar
1 cup granulated sugar	1 teaspoon baking soda
1 cup packed brown sugar	1 teaspoon salt
2 eggs	3 cups old fashioned or quick
1 teaspoon vanilla	oats, uncooked
1½ cups flour	1 cup chopped nuts

Cream margarine and sugars until light and fluffy. Blend in eggs and vanilla. Add combined flour, cream of tartar, baking soda and salt; mix well. Stir in oats and nuts. Chill 1 hour. Shape dough into two rolls, 1½ inches in diameter. Wrap securely; freeze. Cut rolls into ½-inch slices; place, 2½ inches apart, on ungreased cookie sheet. Bake at 350°, 10 to 12 minutes or until lightly browned.

Approximately 7½ dozen

An ideal after-school treat for active youngsters! Store these crunchy favorites in a cookie jar with a loose-fitting lid.

Chocolate Fudge Cookies

1 cup packed brown sugar	1 teaspoon vanilla
½ cup Squeeze Parkay margarine	2½ cups flour
	½ teaspoon baking soda
3 1-oz. squares unsweetened chocolate, melted	¼ teaspoon salt
	½ cup buttermilk
1 egg	

Combine sugar, margarine, chocolate, egg and vanilla; mix well. Add combined dry ingredients alternately with buttermilk, mixing well after each addition. Drop rounded teaspoonfuls of dough onto ungreased cookie sheet. Bake at 350°, 10 to 12 minutes or until tops are slightly cracked.

Approximately 4½ dozen

Coffee Cookies

1 cup Parkay margarine	1½ cups flour
¾ cup sifted confectioners' sugar	1 tablespoon instant coffee granules
½ teaspoon vanilla	Cocoa Frosting

Cream margarine and sugar until light and fluffy. Blend in vanilla. Add combined flour and coffee granules; mix well. Chill. Shape dough into 1-inch balls; place on ungreased cookie sheet. Bake at 350°, 15 to 20 minutes or until lightly browned. Cool; frost with:

Cocoa Frosting

| 2 tablespoons Parkay margarine | 1½ tablespoons cocoa |
| 1¾ cups sifted confectioners' sugar | 2 tablespoons milk |

Cream margarine. Add combined sugar and cocoa alternately with milk, beating until light and fluffy.

Approximately 3 dozen

Pastel Spritz

1½ cups Parkay margarine	1 egg
1 cup sugar	1 teaspoon vanilla
1 3-oz. pkg. strawberry flavored gelatin	3½ cups flour
	1 teaspoon baking powder

Cream margarine, sugar and gelatin until light and fluffy. Blend in egg and vanilla. Add combined dry ingredients; mix well. Force dough through cookie press onto ungreased cookie sheet. Bake at 400°, 8 to 10 minutes or until edges are very lightly browned.

Approximately 10 dozen

Variation: Substitute any flavored gelatin for strawberry.

Coffee Cookies, Pastel Spritz, Carousel Cookies (page 54), Festive Lemon Bars (page 54)

Carousel Cookies

1 cup Parkay margarine
¼ cup sugar
1 teaspoon almond extract
½ teaspoon salt

2 cups flour
1 cup chopped nuts
Kraft strawberry or red
    raspberry preserves

Cream margarine and sugar until light and fluffy. Blend in almond extract. Add combined flour and salt; mix well. Shape level tablespoonfuls of dough into balls; roll in nuts. Place on ungreased cookie sheet; flatten slightly. Indent centers; fill with preserves. Bake at 400°, 10 to 12 minutes or just until lightly browned.

Approximately 2½ dozen

Festive Lemon Bars

Flour
Sifted confectioners' sugar
½ cup Parkay margarine
1 cup granulated sugar

3 eggs, slightly beaten
½ teaspoon baking powder
½ cup lemon juice

Combine 1 cup flour and ¼ cup confectioners' sugar; cut in margarine until mixture resembles coarse crumbs. Press onto bottom of 9-inch square pan. Bake at 350°, 15 minutes. Combine 2 tablespoons flour, granulated sugar, eggs and baking powder; mix well. Stir in lemon juice. Pour over crust; continue baking 25 minutes. Cool. Sprinkle with additional confectioners' sugar; cut into bars.

Choco-Nut Cookies

1 cup Parkay margarine
1 cup sifted confectioners'
    sugar
¼ cup milk
1 egg

1 teaspoon vanilla
3 cups flour
½ cup cocoa
¼ teaspoon salt
1 cup finely chopped pecans

Cream margarine and sugar until light and fluffy. Blend in milk, egg and vanilla. Add combined dry ingredients; mix well. Stir in nuts. Shape dough into two rolls, 1½ inches in diameter. Wrap securely; chill several hours. Cut rolls into ⅛-inch slices; place on ungreased cookie sheet. Bake at 400°, 8 to 10 minutes.

Approximately 5½ dozen

Kolacky Cookies

1 cup Parkay margarine	1 teaspoon grated lemon rind
1 8-oz. pkg. Philadelphia Brand cream cheese	2½ cups flour
2 tablespoons sugar	2 teaspoons baking powder
2 eggs, separated	½ teaspoon salt
1 teaspoon vanilla	Kraft strawberry preserves

Combine margarine, softened cream cheese and sugar, mixing until well blended. Blend in egg yolks, vanilla and lemon rind. Add combined dry ingredients; mix well. Chill. On lightly floured surface, roll out dough to ¼-inch thickness; cut with 2-inch round cookie cutter. Place on ungreased cookie sheet; brush with egg white. Indent centers; fill with preserves. Bake at 350°, 15 minutes.

Approximately 4 dozen

Variation: Substitute any flavor preserves or marmalade for strawberry preserves.

A European classic, Kolacky are great attractions at fund raising bazaars and cookie exchanges.

Snickerdoodles

1 cup Parkay margarine	2 teaspoons cream of tartar
Sugar	1 teaspoon baking soda
2 eggs	½ teaspoon salt
2¾ cups flour	1 tablespoon cinnamon

Cream margarine and 1½ cups sugar until light and fluffy. Blend in eggs. Add combined flour, cream of tartar, baking soda and salt; mix well. Chill. Shape rounded teaspoonfuls of dough into balls; roll in combined 3 tablespoons sugar and cinnamon. Place, 2 inches apart, on ungreased cookie sheet. Bake at 400°, 10 to 12 minutes or until lightly browned.

Approximately 5½ dozen

Hawaiian Nut Cookies

⅓ cup Parkay margarine
½ cup packed brown sugar
¼ cup granulated sugar
1 egg
1 teaspoon vanilla
1¾ cups flour

½ teaspoon baking powder
½ teaspoon baking soda
¼ teaspoon salt
1 8¼-oz. can crushed
   pineapple, drained
½ cup chopped nuts

Cream margarine and sugars until light and fluffy. Blend in egg and vanilla. Add combined dry ingredients; mix well. Stir in pineapple and nuts. Drop rounded teaspoonfuls of dough onto greased cookie sheet. Bake at 400°, 10 to 12 minutes or until golden brown.

Approximately 3 dozen

Variation: Substitute ¾ cup shredded coconut for nuts.

A delightful party cookie with tropical appeal!

Cinnamon Apple Drop Cookies

½ cup Parkay margarine
1 cup packed brown sugar
1 egg
1 teaspoon vanilla
2½ cups flour
½ teaspoon baking powder

½ teaspoon baking soda
½ teaspoon salt
½ teaspoon cinnamon
2 cups finely chopped
   peeled apples

Cream margarine and sugar until light and fluffy. Blend in egg and vanilla. Add combined dry ingredients; mix well. Stir in apples. Drop rounded teaspoonfuls of dough onto ungreased cookie sheet. Bake at 350°, 20 minutes.

Approximately 4 dozen

Variation: Add ½ cup chopped walnuts or pecans.

Use tart, firm cooking apples such as Winesap, McIntosh, Jonathan or Rome Beauty.

Marble Squares

1 8-oz. pkg. Philadelphia
  Brand cream cheese
2⅓ cups sugar
3 eggs
¾ cup water
½ cup Parkay margarine
1½ 1-oz. squares unsweetened
  chocolate

2 cups flour
½ cup dairy sour cream
1 teaspoon baking soda
½ teaspoon salt
1 6-oz. pkg. semi-sweet
  chocolate pieces

Combine softened cream cheese and ⅓ cup sugar, mixing until well blended. Blend in 1 egg. Combine water, margarine and chocolate in saucepan; bring to boil. Remove from heat. Stir in combined remaining sugar and flour. Add remaining eggs, sour cream, baking soda and salt; mix well. Pour into greased and floured 15½×10½-inch jelly roll pan. Spoon cream cheese mixture over chocolate batter. Cut through batter with knife several times for marble effect. Sprinkle with chocolate pieces. Bake at 375°, 25 to 30 minutes or until wooden pick inserted in center comes out clean. Cool; cut into squares.

Pecan Caramel Bars

⅔ cup Parkay margarine
½ cup packed brown sugar
1½ cups flour
   *   *   *
28 Kraft caramels
¼ cup Parkay margarine

¼ cup water
2 eggs, slightly beaten
¼ cup granulated sugar
½ teaspoon vanilla
¼ teaspoon salt
1 cup chopped pecans

Cream margarine and brown sugar until light and fluffy. Add flour; mix well. Press onto bottom of 13×9-inch baking pan. Bake at 375°, 15 minutes. Melt caramels with margarine and water in saucepan over low heat; stir occasionally until smooth. Combine eggs, granulated sugar, vanilla and salt. Gradually add caramel sauce; mix well. Stir in nuts. Pour over crust; continue baking 15 minutes. Cool; cut into bars.

Molasses Crinkles

¾ cup Parkay margarine
1 cup packed brown sugar
¼ cup molasses
1 egg
2¼ cups flour
2 teaspoons baking soda

1 teaspoon cinnamon
1 teaspoon ginger
½ teaspoon ground cloves
¼ teaspoon salt
Granulated sugar

Cream margarine and brown sugar until light and fluffy. Blend in molasses and egg. Add combined flour, baking soda, spices and salt; mix well. Chill 1 hour. Shape rounded tablespoonfuls of dough into balls; dip in granulated sugar. Place 3 inches apart on greased cookie sheet, sugar-side up. Bake at 375°, 10 to 12 minutes. Remove from cookie sheet immediately.

Approximately 2½ dozen

Checkerboard Cookies

½ cup Parkay margarine
¾ cup sugar
1 egg
1 teaspoon vanilla
2 cups flour

1 teaspoon baking powder
½ teaspoon salt
1 1-oz. square unsweetened
  chocolate, melted

Cream margarine and sugar until light and fluffy. Blend in egg and vanilla. Add combined dry ingredients; mix well. Divide dough in half; blend chocolate into one half. Shape each portion into 2-inch square bar; cut in half lengthwise. Press one chocolate and one plain half together to form square bar. Cut in half lengthwise again; press halves together to form checkerboard pattern. Repeat with remaining halves. Wrap securely; chill. Cut rolls into ¼-inch slices; place on ungreased cookie sheet. Bake at 375°, 8 to 10 minutes or until edges are lightly browned.

Approximately 3 dozen

Molasses Crinkles, Checkerboard Cookies, Marble Squares (page 57),
Pecan Caramel Bars (page 57)

Queen's Lace Cookies

¼ cup Squeeze Parkay
    margarine
¼ cup granulated sugar
2 tablespoons dark corn syrup
1 teaspoon brandy

½ cup flour
½ teaspoon grated lemon rind
¼ teaspoon ginger
Brandied Whipped Cream

Heat margarine, granulated sugar and corn syrup over low heat in heavy skillet or saucepan, stirring until sugar is dissolved. Remove from heat; beat in brandy and combined flour, lemon rind and ginger. Drop level teaspoonfuls of batter, 3 inches apart, onto greased cookie sheet. Bake at 350°, 8 to 10 minutes or until deep golden brown. Remove from oven; wait 10 to 15 seconds for cookie to set. Remove cookies one at a time; turn smooth-side up and wrap around handle of a wooden spoon spread with margarine. Slip cookie off; repeat with remaining cookies, working quickly. If cookies become too firm to roll, return to oven for 1 to 2 minutes to soften. When ready to serve, fill cookies with:

Brandied Whipped Cream

1 cup heavy cream
2 tablespoons confectioners'
    sugar

1 tablespoon brandy

Whip cream until slightly thickened; gradually add sugar and brandy, beating until stiff peaks form.

Approximately 1½ dozen

Crisp, spicy cookies with a delicate cream filling - an elegant dessert for dinner parties, receptions and other formal occasions.

Peanut-Jelly Bars

¾ cup Parkay margarine
1 cup packed brown sugar
1½ cups flour
1 teaspoon salt
½ teaspoon baking soda

1½ cups old fashioned or quick
    oats, uncooked
½ cup chopped peanuts
1 10-oz. jar Kraft grape jelly

Cream margarine and sugar until light and fluffy. Add combined flour, salt and baking soda; mix well. Stir in oats and nuts. Press half of crumb mixture onto bottom of greased 13×9-inch baking pan; spread with jelly. Cover with remaining crumb mixture. Bake at 400°, 25 minutes. Cool; cut into bars.

Spicy Thins

1 cup Parkay margarine
1½ cups sugar
1 egg
2 tablespoons dark corn syrup
3 cups flour

2 teaspoons baking soda
2 teaspoons cinnamon
2 teaspoons ginger
2 teaspoons ground cloves

Cream margarine and sugar until light and fluffy. Blend in egg and corn syrup. Add combined dry ingredients; mix well. Chill. On lightly floured surface, roll out dough to ⅛-inch thickness; cut with assorted 3-inch cookie cutters. Place on greased cookie sheet. Bake at 400°, 6 to 8 minutes or until edges are very lightly browned.

Approximately 6½ dozen

Crunchies

½ cup Parkay margarine
¾ cup packed brown sugar
1 egg
1 teaspoon vanilla

1¼ cups flour
½ teaspoon baking powder
¼ teaspoon salt
2 cups crisp rice cereal

Cream margarine and sugar until light and fluffy. Blend in egg and vanilla. Add combined flour, baking powder and salt; mix well. Stir in cereal. Drop rounded teaspoonfuls of dough onto greased cookie sheet. Bake at 375°, 8 to 10 minutes or until golden brown.

Approximately 3 dozen

Banana-Coconut Cookies

1¾ cups old fashioned or quick
    oats, uncooked
1½ cups flour
1 cup sugar
1 teaspoon salt
½ teaspoon baking soda
1 cup mashed bananas

¾ cup Squeeze Parkay
    margarine
½ cup shredded coconut,
    toasted
1 egg, slightly beaten
½ teaspoon vanilla

Combine dry ingredients. Add remaining ingredients; mix well. Drop rounded teaspoonfuls of dough, 2 inches apart, onto ungreased cookie sheet. Bake at 350°, 12 to 15 minutes or until edges are golden brown.

Approximately 4 dozen

Variation: Substitute chopped walnuts or pecans for coconut.

Bananas should be very ripe for optimum flavor.

Cookie Storage Tips

Knowing the proper way to keep your cookies fresh is important and varies with the type. Here are the rules to follow:

- Soft cookies should be kept in a container with a tight-fitting cover. A bread slice or an apple wedge will add extra moisture to keep cookies even softer.

- Crisp cookies are best stored in a container with a loose-fitting lid. If they do soften, place in a 300° oven for about 5 minutes.

- Bar cookies can be stored tightly covered in their baking pan.

- Cookies and bars can be wrapped securely in moisture-vaporproof wrap and stored in the freezer up to 6 months.

Cookies to Travel

Some cookies travel better than others — avoid crisp, fragile cookies that crumble easily. Whatever the destination, follow these simple steps to assure safe arrival.

- Use a sturdy container such as a metal coffee can with a plastic lid.

- Line mailing container with foil or plastic wrap.

- Wrap 4 or 5 cookies of same size together in foil or plastic wrap and seal with tape.

- Place heaviest cookies on bottom and layer with cushioning materials such as shredded paper or crumbled waxed paper.

- Seal container securely with tape.

- Mark outside wrapping "Perishable — Food" to help assure that the package receives more rapid and careful routing.

Extra Special Cakes

Cake baking and decorating is always fun and rewarding, especially when the selection of recipes is so varied and inviting. Coconut Sour Cream Cake, Company Pumpkin Squares and Orange Kuchen are just a few of the extra special selections offered here.

Cake Baking Tips

- Use all-purpose flour unless recipe indicates cake flour.

- Push batter to sides of cake pans; then gently tap pans on counter to remove air bubbles.

- Center single cake pans on oven rack. Allow space between two pans. Stagger cake pans that must be placed on two shelves.

- Let cakes cool in pans 10 minutes before removing or as recipe indicates.

Frosting Tips

- Cool cake completely before decorating unless recipe specifies otherwise.

- To split layers, mark even widths along side of cake with picks. Draw a piece of thread through cake, following markers, or cut with a long sharp knife.

- Lightly brush cake to remove excess crumbs.

- For two-layer cakes, the bottom layer should be upside-down and the top layer right-side up, for best shape and easier frosting.

- Fill cake layers with about ½ cup frosting.

- Carefully spread a thin layer of frosting on the sides of the cake to set any remaining crumbs before frosting entire cake.

Peach Upside-Down Cake

Parkay margarine
½ cup packed brown sugar
1½ cups fresh peach slices
⅔ cup granulated sugar
1 egg

½ teaspoon vanilla
1½ cups flour
1½ teaspoons baking powder
½ teaspoon salt
½ cup milk

Melt 3 tablespoons margarine in 8 or 9-inch oven-proof skillet or layer pan; sprinkle with brown sugar. Arrange fruit in skillet. Cream ⅓ cup margarine and granulated sugar until light and fluffy. Blend in egg and vanilla. Add combined dry ingredients alternately with milk, mixing well after each addition. Carefully pour batter over fruit. Bake at 350°, 40 to 45 minutes or until wooden pick inserted in center comes out clean. Immediately invert onto serving platter.

Variation: Substitute 16-oz. can peach slices, drained, for fresh peaches.

Glazed Pound Cake

2 cups Parkay margarine
4 cups sifted confectioners' sugar
2 tablespoons grated orange rind

6 eggs
3½ cups flour
½ teaspoon mace
¼ teaspoon salt
Orange Glaze

Cream margarine at medium speed of electric mixer 3 minutes or until light and fluffy. Gradually add sugar and orange rind; cream thoroughly. Add eggs, one at a time, mixing well after each addition. Gradually add combined dry ingredients; mix well. Pour into greased and floured 10-inch tube pan or Bundt pan. Bake at 350°, 1 hour and 10 minutes or until wooden pick inserted in center comes out clean. Remove from pan; cool. Glaze with:

Orange Glaze

2 cups sifted confectioners' sugar

3 tablespoons orange juice

Combine sugar and orange juice; mix well.

Lemon Tea Cakes

½ cup Parkay margarine
½ cup sugar
1 tablespoon grated lemon rind
2 eggs, separated
1 cup flour

1 teaspoon baking powder
¼ teaspoon salt
3 tablespoons lemon juice
Lemon Glaze

Cream margarine and sugar until light and fluffy. Blend in lemon rind. Add egg yolks, one at a time, mixing well after each addition. Add combined dry ingredients alternately with lemon juice, mixing well after each addition. Fold in stiffly beaten egg whites. Spoon into greased medium-size muffin pan, filling each cup ½ full. Bake 375°, 20 to 25 minutes. Cool; glaze with:

Lemon Glaze

1 cup sifted confectioners'
sugar

1½ tablespoons lemon juice

Combine sugar and lemon juice; mix well.

1 dozen

Mincemeat Squares

½ cup Parkay margarine
1 cup packed brown sugar
1 cup ready-to-use mincemeat
2 eggs
1 teaspoon rum flavoring

1½ cups flour
½ teaspoon baking powder
½ teaspoon salt
½ cup chopped nuts
Fluffy Frosting

Cream margarine and sugar until light and fluffy. Blend in mincemeat, eggs and rum flavoring. Add combined dry ingredients; mix well. Stir in nuts. Pour into greased and floured 13×9-inch baking pan. Bake at 350°, 35 to 40 minutes or until wooden pick inserted in center comes out clean. Cool. Frost with Fluffy Frosting; cut into squares.

Fluffy Frosting

⅓ cup Parkay margarine
2 cups sifted confectioners'
sugar

1 tablespoon milk

Cream margarine. Add sugar and milk, beating until light and fluffy.

Applesauce Cake

½ cup Parkay margarine	1½ teaspoons salt
2 cups sugar	1 teaspoon cinnamon
1 15-oz. jar applesauce	½ teaspoon ground cloves
1 egg	½ teaspoon ground allspice
2½ cups flour	1 cup raisins
1½ teaspoons baking soda	

Cream margarine and sugar until light and fluffy. Blend in applesauce and egg. Add combined dry ingredients; mix well. Stir in raisins. Pour into greased and floured 13×9-inch baking pan. Bake at 350°, 45 minutes or until wooden pick inserted in center comes out clean. Cool. Sprinkle with confectioners' sugar, if desired.

Peanut Butter Picnic Cake

½ cup Parkay margarine	1 tablespoon baking powder
1⅓ cups sugar	1 teaspoon salt
¼ cup peanut butter	1 cup milk
2 eggs	1 10-oz. jar Kraft strawberry
1 teaspoon vanilla	preserves or grape jelly
2 cups flour	Peanut Butter Frosting

Cream margarine and sugar until light and fluffy. Blend in peanut butter, eggs and vanilla. Add combined dry ingredients alternately with milk, mixing well after each addition. Pour into two greased and floured 8 or 9-inch layer pans. Bake at 350°, 35 to 40 minutes or until wooden pick inserted in center comes out clean. Cool 10 minutes; remove from pans. Spread ⅔ cup preserves between layers. Frost with Peanut Butter Frosting. Decorate with additional preserves.

Peanut Butter Frosting

¼ cup Parkay margarine	2½ cups sifted confectioners'
¼ cup peanut butter	sugar
1 teaspoon vanilla	3 tablespoons milk
Dash of salt	

Cream margarine; blend in peanut butter, vanilla and salt. Add sugar alternately with milk, beating until light and fluffy.

Cake Café

2/3 cup Parkay margarine
1 1/3 cups sugar
2 eggs
1 teaspoon vanilla
1 teaspoon instant coffee
   granules

2 cups flour
1 tablespoon baking powder
1 teaspoon salt
1 cup milk
   Creamy Mocha Frosting

Cream margarine and sugar until light and fluffy. Blend in eggs, vanilla and coffee granules. Add combined dry ingredients alternately with milk, mixing well after each addition. Pour into two greased and floured 8 or 9-inch layer pans. Bake at 350°, 30 to 35 minutes or until wooden pick inserted in center comes out clean. Cool 10 minutes; remove from pans. Fill and frost with:

Creamy Mocha Frosting

1/2 cup Parkay margarine
2 1-oz. squares unsweetened
   chocolate, melted
2 teaspoons instant coffee
   granules

1 teaspoon vanilla
4 cups sifted confectioners'
   sugar
1/4 cup milk

Cream margarine; blend in chocolate, coffee granules and vanilla. Add sugar alternately with milk, beating until light and fluffy.

In a hurry? Prepare a two-layer yellow or chocolate cake mix as directed on the package. Add instant coffee granules with the eggs. Bake in a 13 × 9-inch baking pan. Frost top with Creamy Mocha Frosting and sprinkle with sliced almonds.

Cake Café, Peanut Butter Picnic Cake (page 69), Coconut Sour Cream Cake (page 72)

Coconut Sour Cream Cake

¾ cup Parkay margarine	¾ teaspoon salt
1½ cups sugar	1¼ cups milk
¾ cup dairy sour cream	1 3½-oz. can flaked
1 teaspoon vanilla	coconut
3 cups sifted cake flour	4 egg whites
2 teaspoons baking powder	Fluffy Vanilla Frosting
¾ teaspoon baking soda	

Cream margarine and sugar until light and fluffy. Blend in sour cream and vanilla. Add combined dry ingredients alternately with milk, mixing well after each addition. Stir in ¾ cup coconut. Fold in stiffly beaten egg whites. Pour into three greased and floured 9-inch layer pans. Bake at 350°, 30 to 35 minutes or until wooden pick inserted in center comes out clean. Cool 10 minutes; remove from pans. Fill and frost with Fluffy Vanilla Frosting; sprinkle with remaining coconut.

Fluffy Vanilla Frosting

¾ cup Parkay margarine	6 cups sifted confectioners'
½ teaspoon vanilla	sugar
Dash of salt	1 egg white
	2 to 3 tablespoons milk

Cream margarine; blend in vanilla and salt. Add sugar alternately with egg white and milk, beating until light and fluffy.

For a festive touch, tint coconut pink or yellow before sprinkling on the cake.

To tint coconut, dilute a few drops of food coloring with ½ teaspoon water in a jar. Add coconut, filling jar half full. Cover and shake.

Peanut Graham Cake

¾ cup Parkay margarine
1 cup sugar
3 eggs, separated
1 teaspoon vanilla
2½ cups (15) crushed graham
crackers

1 cup flour
4 teaspoons baking powder
1 teaspoon salt
1 cup milk
Peanut Creme Frosting

Cream margarine and sugar until light and fluffy. Blend in egg yolks and vanilla. Add combined dry ingredients alternately with milk, mixing well after each addition. Fold in stiffly beaten egg whites. Pour into greased and floured 13×9-inch baking pan. Bake at 350°, 30 minutes or until wooden pick inserted in center comes out clean. Cool; frost with:

Peanut Creme Frosting

¼ cup milk
1 7-oz. jar Kraft marshmallow
creme

½ cup peanut butter

Gradually add milk to marshmallow creme; mix until well blended. Add peanut butter, beating until light and fluffy.

Company Pumpkin Squares

⅔ cup soft Parkay margarine
1½ cups sugar
1 16-oz. can pumpkin
3 eggs
2 cups flour

2 teaspoons pumpkin pie spice
2 teaspoons baking powder
½ teaspoon baking soda
½ teaspoon salt
Vanilla Frosting

Cream margarine and sugar until light and fluffy. Blend in pumpkin and eggs. Add combined dry ingredients; mix well. Pour into greased 15½×10½-inch jelly roll pan. Bake at 350°, 35 to 40 minutes or until wooden pick inserted in center comes out clean. Cool; frost with Vanilla Frosting. Cut into squares.

Vanilla Frosting

⅓ cup soft Parkay margarine
1 teaspoon vanilla
Dash of salt

4½ cups sifted confectioners'
sugar
¼ cup milk

Cream margarine; blend in vanilla and salt. Add sugar alternately with milk, beating until light and fluffy.

Orange Pride Cake

⅔ cup Parkay margarine
1⅓ cups sugar
2 eggs
1 teaspoon vanilla
1 teaspoon grated orange rind
2 cups flour

1 tablespoon baking powder
1 teaspoon salt
1 cup milk
Orange Frosting
½ cup toasted coconut

Cream margarine and sugar until light and fluffy. Blend in eggs, vanilla and orange rind. Add combined dry ingredients alternately with milk, mixing well after each addition. Pour into greased and floured 13×9-inch baking pan. Bake at 350°, 30 to 35 minutes or until wooden pick inserted in center comes out clean. Cool. Frost with Orange Frosting; sprinkle with coconut.

Orange Frosting

⅓ cup Parkay margarine
1 teaspoon grated orange rind
Dash of salt

3 cups sifted confectioners' sugar
3 tablespoons orange juice

Cream margarine; blend in orange rind and salt. Add sugar alternately with orange juice, beating until light and fluffy.

Fudge Ripple Cake

1 cup Parkay margarine
1½ cups sugar
4 eggs
1 teaspoon vanilla
3 cups flour

1 tablespoon baking powder
1 teaspoon salt
1 cup milk
¾ cup Kraft fudge topping
Fudge Glaze

Cream margarine and sugar until light and fluffy. Blend in eggs and vanilla. Add combined dry ingredients alternately with milk, mixing well after each addition. Divide batter in half; blend topping into one half. Pour half of white batter into well-greased and floured 10-inch tube pan or Bundt pan; cover with half of chocolate batter. Repeat layers. Bake at 350°, 50 to 55 minutes or until wooden pick inserted in center comes out clean. Cool 10 minutes; remove from pan. Glaze with:

Fudge Glaze

½ cup sifted confectioners' sugar

¼ cup Kraft fudge topping
1½ teaspoons milk

Combine ingredients; mix well.

Applesauce Cheddar Fruitcake

½ cup Parkay margarine
1 cup sugar
2 eggs
3 cups flour
2 teaspoons baking powder
1 teaspoon cinnamon
½ teaspoon salt
¼ teaspoon nutmeg
1 cup applesauce

1 cup chopped pecans
½ cup chopped dates
½ cup chopped maraschino
  cherries, well-drained
2 cups (8 ozs.) shredded
  Kraft sharp natural cheddar
  cheese
Brandied Sauce

Cream margarine and sugar until light and fluffy. Add eggs, one at a time, mixing well after each addition. Add combined 2 cups flour, baking powder, cinnamon, salt and nutmeg alternately with applesauce, mixing well after each addition. Combine remaining flour, nuts, dates and cherries; stir in cheese. Fold into batter. Pour into well-greased 12-cup ring mold. Bake at 325°, 1 hour. Cool 10 minutes; remove from pan. Cool. Sprinkle with confectioners' sugar and serve with:

Brandied Sauce

1 3-oz. pkg. Philadelphia
  Brand cream cheese
3 tablespoons milk
1 teaspoon brandy flavoring

Dash of salt
2½ cups sifted confectioners'
  sugar

Combine softened cream cheese, milk, brandy flavoring and salt, mixing until well blended. Add sugar, beating until light and fluffy.

Variation: To flavor with brandy, wrap cake in cheesecloth moistened with ½ cup brandy. Wrap securely in heavy duty aluminum foil; store in cool, dry place for 1 week. Moisten cloth with ¼ cup brandy; store 1 week. Repeat.

To cut fruitcake with ease, use a very sharp knife and clean the blade after each slice.

German Chocolate Cake

1 cup Parkay margarine
1⅔ cups sugar
4 eggs, separated
1 4-oz. pkg. sweet chocolate, melted
1 teaspoon vanilla

2¼ cups flour
2 teaspoons baking powder
½ teaspoon salt
1¼ cups milk
Coconut Topping

Cream margarine and sugar until light and fluffy. Blend in egg yolks, chocolate and vanilla. Add combined dry ingredients alternately with milk, mixing well after each addition. Fold in stiffly beaten egg whites. Pour into three greased and floured 9-inch layer pans. Bake at 350°, 25 to 30 minutes or until wooden pick inserted in center comes out clean. Cool 10 minutes; remove from pans. Frost top of each layer with Coconut Topping; stack layers.

Coconut Topping

½ cup Parkay margarine
½ cup packed brown sugar
½ cup milk
2 eggs, slightly beaten

2 cups chopped pecans
2 cups flaked coconut
2 teaspoons vanilla

Combine margarine, sugar, milk and eggs in saucepan. Cook over low heat, stirring constantly, until thickened. Stir in remaining ingredients.

Orange Kuchen

1 cup Parkay margarine
2 cups sugar
2 tablespoons grated orange rind
1½ teaspoons vanilla
4 eggs, separated

3 cups flour
2½ teaspoons baking powder
¾ teaspoon salt
½ cup orange juice
½ cup milk
Orange Glaze

Cream margarine and sugar until light and fluffy. Blend in orange rind and vanilla. Add egg yolks, one at a time, mixing well after each addition. Add combined dry ingredients alternately with juice and milk, mixing well after each addition. Fold in stiffly beaten egg whites. Pour into greased and floured 10-inch tube pan or Bundt pan. Bake at 350°, 55 to 60 minutes or until wooden pick inserted in center comes out clean. Cool 10 minutes; remove from pan. Glaze with Orange Glaze (page 77).

Orange Glaze

2 cups sifted confectioners'
  sugar
2 tablespoons orange juice

¼ teaspoon vanilla
Dash of salt

Combine ingredients; mix well.

Variation: Omit glaze. Decorate cake by sifting confectioners'
  sugar over a paper doily placed on top of cake.
  Carefully remove doily.

Banana 'N Spice Cake

2½ cups flour
  1 cup granulated sugar
  1 cup mashed bananas
  ½ cup Squeeze Parkay
    margarine
  ½ cup packed brown sugar
  ½ cup chopped walnuts

2 teaspoons baking powder
1 teaspoon salt
½ teaspoon cinnamon
¼ teaspoon nutmeg
2 eggs
Easy Vanilla Frosting

Combine ingredients except Easy Vanilla Frosting, mixing just
until moistened. Pour into a greased and floured 13×9-inch
baking pan. Bake at 350°, 40 to 45 minutes or until wooden pick
inserted in center comes out clean. Cool; frost with:

Easy Vanilla Frosting

½ cup Squeeze Parkay
  margarine
1 teaspoon vanilla
  Dash of salt

4 cups sifted confectioners'
  sugar
2 tablespoons milk

Combine margarine, vanilla and salt. Add sugar and milk,
beating until light and fluffy.

Variations: Substitute one of the following for bananas:

- 8¼-oz. can crushed pineapple, undrained
- 16-oz. can apricots, drained, chopped
- 1 cup applesauce

Black Forest Torte

1¼ cups sugar
⅔ cup Squeeze Parkay margarine
3 eggs
3 1-oz. squares unsweetened
   chocolate, melted
1 teaspoon vanilla
1¾ cups flour

1 teaspoon baking powder
1 teaspoon baking soda
1 teaspoon salt
⅔ cup buttermilk
Chocolate Filling
Brandied Cherry Filling
Whipped Cream Frosting

Combine sugar and margarine. Add eggs, one at a time, mixing well after each addition. Blend in chocolate and vanilla. Add combined dry ingredients alternately with buttermilk, mixing well after each addition. Pour into two greased and floured 8-inch layer pans. Bake at 350°, 30 to 35 minutes or until wooden pick inserted in center comes out clean. Cool 10 minutes; remove from pans. Cool; split each layer in half horizontally. Spread one layer with Chocolate Filling; top with second layer spread with Brandied Cherry Filling. Repeat with remaining layers. Frost sides of cake with Whipped Cream Frosting.

Chocolate Filling

1 cup heavy cream
¼ cup confectioners' sugar

1 tablespoon cocoa
½ teaspoon vanilla

Beat cream until slightly thickened; gradually add sugar, cocoa and vanilla, beating until stiff peaks form.

Brandied Cherry Filling

1 16-oz. can pitted sour
   cherries or 1 16-oz. pkg.
   frozen sour cherries,
   thawed

2 tablespoons cornstarch
¼ cup sugar
2 tablespoons brandy

Drain cherries, reserving ¾ cup syrup. Combine cornstarch and sugar in saucepan; gradually add reserved syrup. Cook over medium heat until mixture is clear and thickened. Stir in cherries and brandy. Cool.

Whipped Cream Frosting

1 cup heavy cream
¼ cup confectioners'
   sugar

½ teaspoon vanilla

Beat cream until slightly thickened; gradually add sugar and vanilla, beating until stiff peaks form.

Gingerbread with Lemon Sauce

½ cup Squeeze Parkay
   margarine
½ cup packed brown sugar
2 eggs
1 cup boiling water
½ cup dark molasses
2 cups flour
1½ teaspoons baking powder

1½ teaspoons ginger
1½ teaspoons cinnamon
½ teaspoon baking soda
½ teaspoon salt
½ teaspoon nutmeg
⅛ teaspoon ground cloves
Lemon Sauce

Combine margarine and sugar. Blend in eggs. Stir in boiling water and molasses. Add combined dry ingredients; mix well. Pour into greased 9-inch square pan. Bake at 350°, 45 minutes. Serve with:

Lemon Sauce

⅓ cup sugar
1 tablespoon cornstarch
Dash of salt
¾ cup water

¼ cup Squeeze Parkay
   margarine
3 tablespoons lemon juice
1 tablespoon grated lemon
   rind

Combine sugar, cornstarch and salt in saucepan; gradually add water. Cook over medium heat until mixture is clear and thickened. Remove from heat; stir in remaining ingredients. Serve hot or cold over gingerbread.

Variations: Omit Lemon Sauce: Top servings with vanilla ice cream and crushed pineapple.

Add ½ cup chopped walnuts to batter. Serve gingerbread warm with hot applesauce and whipped cream.

Versatile gingerbread is an old fashioned specialty for family meals, guest dinners or entertaining. The gingerbread can be prepared in advance, securely wrapped in foil and frozen. To thaw, loosen the wrapping and let stand at room temperature.

Nutty Carrot Cake

1 cup Parkay margarine	2 teaspoons cinnamon
1½ cups sugar	¾ teaspoon baking soda
2 cups finely shredded carrots	¾ teaspoon salt
3 eggs	½ cup milk
1 teaspoon vanilla	½ cup chopped nuts
2½ cups flour	Vanilla "Philly" Frosting
2 teaspoons baking powder	

Cream margarine and sugar until light and fluffy. Blend in carrots, eggs and vanilla. Add combined dry ingredients alternately with milk, mixing well after each addition. Stir in nuts. Pour into greased 13×9-inch baking pan. Bake at 350°, 45 to 50 minutes or until wooden pick inserted in center comes out clean. Cool; frost with Vanilla "Philly" Frosting. Garnish with additional chopped nuts, if desired.

Vanilla "Philly" Frosting

1 3-oz. pkg. Philadelphia	½ teaspoon vanilla
Brand cream cheese	3 cups sifted confectioners'
1 tablespoon milk	sugar

Combine softened cream cheese, milk and vanilla, mixing until well blended. Gradually add sugar, beating until light and fluffy.

Variations: Substitute shredded zucchini for carrots.

Omit frosting. Serve with vanilla ice cream and Kraft artificially flavored butterscotch topping.

Nutty Carrot Cake is a favorite for picnics, potluck suppers and other casual gatherings. It is a moist spicy cake that stays fresh for days. A baking pan with a tight-fitting cover is ideal for storing cakes.

Chocolate Coconut Cake

⅔ cup Parkay margarine	4 teaspoons baking powder
1⅓ cups sugar	1 teaspoon salt
2 eggs	1½ cups milk
1 teaspoon vanilla	¾ cup flaked coconut
2 cups flour	Angel Mallow Frosting
½ cup cocoa	

Cream margarine and sugar until light and fluffy. Blend in eggs and vanilla. Add combined dry ingredients alternately with milk, mixing well after each addition. Stir in coconut. Pour into two greased and floured 9-inch layer pans. Bake at 350°, 30 to 35 minutes or until wooden pick inserted in center comes out clean. Cool 10 minutes; remove from pans. Fill and frost with:

Angel Mallow Frosting

½ cup sugar	1 7-oz. jar Kraft marshmallow
2 egg whites	creme
2 tablespoons water	½ teaspoon vanilla

Combine sugar, egg whites and water in double boiler; beat with electric or rotary beater over boiling water until soft peaks form. Add marshmallow creme; continue beating until stiff peaks form. Remove from heat; beat in vanilla. Tint pink with red food coloring, if desired.

Desserts Too Good To Be True

Simple or fancy, hot or cold, family favorites and party spectaculars—these delicious desserts are festive finales for any meal. They can also be served solo for entertaining.

Apple Pizza Pie

¾ cup Parkay margarine
1 cup packed brown sugar
1 egg
1½ cups flour
1½ cups old fashioned or quick
   oats, uncooked
6 cups apple slices

*   *   *

¼ cup flour
2 tablespoons sugar
1 teaspoon cinnamon
¼ teaspoon nutmeg
2 tablespoons Parkay
   margarine

Cream margarine and sugar until light and fluffy. Blend in egg. Add combined dry ingredients; mix well. Spread into greased 14-inch pizza pan. Arrange apples on batter.

Combine dry ingredients; cut in margarine until mixture resembles coarse crumbs. Sprinkle over apples. Bake at 400°, 30 to 35 minutes or until apples are tender. Cut into wedges. Serve warm or cold.

Variation: Substitute 15½×10½-inch jelly roll pan for pizza pan.

Cranberry Pear Cobbler

1½ cups flour
1½ teaspoons baking powder
¼ teaspoon salt
¼ cup Parkay margarine
1½ cups (6 ozs.) shredded Kraft
   sharp natural cheddar
   cheese
1 egg, slightly beaten
⅓ cup milk

*   *   *

6 cups pear slices
2 cups cranberries
1 tablespoon lemon juice
¾ cup packed brown sugar
3 tablespoons quick-cooking
   tapioca
1 teaspoon cinnamon
¼ teaspoon ginger
¼ teaspoon salt

Combine dry ingredients; cut in margarine until mixture resembles coarse crumbs. Stir in cheese. Add combined egg and milk while mixing lightly with a fork; form into a ball. On lightly floured surface, roll out two-thirds of dough to 15-inch square. Place in 8-inch square baking dish.

Combine fruit and juice. Add combined remaining ingredients; toss lightly. Spoon into pastry shell. Roll out remaining dough to 12-inch square; cut into ½-inch strips. Place strips diagonally across fruit to form lattice; press edges to seal. Flute edges. Bake at 400°, 35 to 40 minutes or until pears are tender.

8 to 10 servings

Dreamy Fruit Tarts

1 cup flour	2 tablespoons cornstarch
¼ teaspoon salt	Dash of salt
1 8-oz. pkg. Philadelphia	1 cup milk
Brand cream cheese	½ teaspoon vanilla
⅔ cup Parkay margarine	Strawberry halves
* * *	Banana slices
½ cup sugar	

Combine flour and salt; cut in 4 ozs. cream cheese and margarine until mixture resembles coarse crumbs. Shape dough into twelve balls; chill. On lightly floured surface, roll out each ball to 4½-inch circle. Place in 3-inch tart pans; prick with fork. Bake at 375°, 15 to 20 minutes or until golden brown. Cool.

Combine sugar, cornstarch and salt in saucepan; gradually add milk. Cook over medium heat, stirring constantly, until clear and thickened. Add the remaining cream cheese, cubed, and vanilla; stir until smooth. Fill tart shells. Chill. Garnish with strawberries and bananas before serving.

German Apple Pancake

2 eggs	1 cup packed brown sugar
½ cup flour	2 tablespoons cornstarch
½ teaspoon salt	½ cup milk
½ cup milk	¼ cup Squeeze Parkay
1 tablespoon Squeeze Parkay	margarine
margarine	4 cups peeled apple slices
* * *	

Combine eggs, flour, salt and milk; beat until smooth. Heat 10-inch oven-proof skillet at 450°, 5 minutes or until hot. Add margarine to coat skillet; pour in batter immediately. Bake at 450°, 10 minutes. Reduce oven temperature to 350°; continue baking 10 minutes or until golden brown.

Combine sugar and cornstarch in saucepan; gradually add milk and margarine. Cook over medium heat, stirring constantly, until mixture is clear and thickened. Reduce heat; stir in apples. Continue cooking until apples are tender. Spoon approximately half of sauce into pancake. Cut into wedges; serve with remaining sauce.

4 to 6 servings

Banana Puff à la Ronde

1 cup water	1 3¾-oz. pkg. vanilla
½ cup soft Parkay margarine	instant pudding mix
1 cup flour	2 cups whipped topping
¼ teaspoon salt	1 banana, sliced
4 eggs	Kraft fudge topping, heated

*   *   *

Bring water and margarine to a boil. Add flour and salt; stir vigorously over low heat until mixture forms a ball. Remove from heat. Add eggs, one at a time, beating well after each addition. Shape into 9-inch ring on ungreased cookie sheet. Bake at 400°, 50 to 55 minutes or until golden brown. Remove from cookie sheet; cool.

Prepare mix as directed for pudding on package. Fold in whipped topping and bananas. Cut top from ring; fill with pudding mixture. Replace top. Chill. Spoon topping over puff when ready to serve. Slice; serve with additional topping.

10 to 12 servings

Caramel Peanut Pie

36 Kraft caramels	½ teaspoon vanilla
¼ cup water	¼ teaspoon salt
¼ cup Parkay margarine	1 cup cocktail peanuts
3 eggs, slightly beaten	1 9-inch unbaked pastry shell
¾ cup sugar	

Melt caramels with water and margarine in saucepan over low heat; stir frequently until smooth. Combine eggs, sugar, vanilla and salt. Gradually add caramel sauce; mix well. Stir in nuts; pour into pastry shell. Bake at 350°, 45 to 50 minutes. Pie filling will appear to be very soft, but becomes firm as it cools.

Bavarian Apple Torte

½ cup Parkay margarine
⅓ cup sugar
¼ teaspoon vanilla
1 cup flour
     *   *   *
1 8-oz. pkg. Philadelphia
    Brand cream cheese
¼ cup sugar

1 egg
½ teaspoon vanilla
     *   *   *
4 cups thin peeled apple
    slices
⅓ cup sugar
½ teaspoon cinnamon
¼ cup sliced almonds

Cream margarine and sugar until light and fluffy. Blend in vanilla. Add flour; mix well. Spread onto bottom and sides of 9-inch springform pan.

Combine softened cream cheese and sugar, mixing until well blended. Blend in egg and vanilla. Pour into pastry-lined pan.

Toss apples with combined sugar and cinnamon; spoon over cream cheese layer. Sprinkle with nuts. Bake at 450°, 10 minutes. Reduce oven temperature to 400°; continue baking 25 minutes. Loosen crust from rim of pan; cool before removing rim of pan.

8 to 10 servings

Mocha Mallow Cheesecake

1 cup chocolate wafer crumbs
⅓ cup Parkay margarine, melted
4 cups Kraft miniature
    marshmallows
⅓ cup milk
1 tablespoon instant coffee
    granules

2 8-oz. pkgs. Philadelphia
    Brand cream cheese
¼ cup sugar
1 teaspoon vanilla
1 cup heavy cream, whipped
2 tablespoons Kraft chocolate
    flavored topping

Combine crumbs and margarine; press onto bottom of 9-inch springform pan. Melt marshmallows with milk and coffee granules in saucepan over low heat; stir occasionally until smooth. Chill until thickened. Mix until well blended. Combine softened cream cheese, sugar and vanilla, mixing until well blended. Add marshmallow mixture; mix well. Fold in whipped cream; pour into crust. Spoon topping over cheesecake mixture. Cut through mixture with knife several times for marble effect. Chill.

Caramel Crunch Apple Pie

28 Kraft caramels
2 tablespoons water
4 cups peeled apple slices
1 9-inch unbaked pastry shell
¾ cup flour

⅓ cup sugar
½ teaspoon cinnamon
⅓ cup Parkay margarine
½ cup chopped walnuts

Melt caramels with water in saucepan over low heat; stir frequently until smooth. Layer apples and caramel sauce in pastry shell. Combine dry ingredients; cut in margarine until mixture resembles coarse crumbs. Stir in nuts. Sprinkle over apples. Bake at 375°, 40 to 45 minutes or until apples are tender.

Marshmallow Crispy Treats

¼ cup Parkay margarine
4 cups Kraft miniature
    marshmallows

5 cups crisp rice cereal

Melt margarine in 3-quart saucepan over low heat. Add marshmallows; stir occasionally until smooth. Remove from heat. Stir in cereal until well coated; press into greased 13×9-inch baking pan. Cool; cut into squares.

Variations: Add 1 cup chopped gumdrops.

Add 1 cup mixed diced candied fruit.

Peachy Dessert Crisp

6 cups peeled peach slices
¾ cup packed brown sugar
½ cup flour
¼ teaspoon nutmeg

¼ teaspoon salt
⅓ cup Parkay margarine
½ cup old fashioned or quick
    oats, uncooked

Place peaches in 9-inch square pan. Combine sugar, flour, nutmeg and salt; cut in margarine until mixture resembles coarse crumbs. Stir in oats. Sprinkle over peaches. Bake at 350°, 40 minutes. Serve warm.

6 to 8 servings

Swedish Pancakes

1 16-oz. can sour pitted
cherries
⅓ cup sugar
2 tablespoons cornstarch
½ teaspoon grated lemon rind
1 tablespoon Squeeze Parkay
margarine

1 cup flour
1 tablespoon sugar
½ teaspoon salt
3 eggs, slightly beaten
2 cups milk
⅓ cup Squeeze Parkay
margarine

*   *   *

Drain cherries, reserving syrup. Add enough water to measure
1¼ cups. Combine sugar, cornstarch and lemon rind in
saucepan; gradually add reserved liquid. Cook over medium
heat, stirring constantly, until mixture is clear and thickened.
Reduce heat; stir in cherries and margarine.

Combine dry ingredients; add eggs, milk and margarine,
beating until smooth. For each pancake, pour ¼ cup batter into
moderately hot, greased 10-inch skillet. Cook until bubbly;
turn. Roll up; serve with cherry sauce.

6 to 8 servings

Austrian Jam Torte

2 cups flour
½ teaspoon baking powder
¼ teaspoon salt
½ cup Parkay margarine
1 egg, beaten

1 tablespoon water
½ teaspoon almond extract
1 10-oz. jar Kraft red
raspberry or strawberry
preserves

Combine dry ingredients; cut in margarine until mixture
resembles coarse crumbs. Add egg, water and almond extract
while mixing lightly with a fork. Chill one quarter of dough.
Press remaining dough onto bottom and ½ inch high around
sides of 9-inch springform pan. Spread dough with preserves.
On lightly floured surface, roll out chilled dough; cut into ½-
inch wide strips. Place strips diagonally across preserves to form
lattice; press edges to seal. Bake at 350°, 35 to 40 minutes or until lightly browned. Loosen crust from rim of pan; cool before
removing rim of pan.

8 to 10 servings

Confetti Mallow Popcorn Balls

4 cups Kraft miniature
   marshmallows
½ cup Parkay margarine
½ teaspoon vanilla

¼ teaspoon salt
3 qts. unsalted popped corn
1½ cups chopped gumdrops

Melt marshmallows with margarine in saucepan over low heat; stir occasionally until smooth. Stir in vanilla and salt. Pour over combined popped corn and gumdrops; toss lightly until well coated. With hands slightly moistened with water, shape into 1½-inch balls; place on greased cookie sheet.

3 dozen

Variations: Substitute 1 cup chopped peanuts or pecans.

           Substitute 1 cup raisins.

Metropolitan Cheesecake

⅓ cup Parkay margarine
⅓ cup sugar
1 egg
1¼ cups flour
    *   *   *
3 8-oz. pkgs. Philadelphia
   Brand cream cheese
¾ cup sugar

1 tablespoon lemon juice
1 teaspoon grated lemon rind
3 eggs
    *   *   *
1 cup dairy sour cream
2 tablespoons sugar
1 teaspoon vanilla
Fresh fruit

Cream margarine and sugar until light and fluffy. Blend in egg. Add flour; mix well. Spread dough onto bottom and 1½ inches high around sides of 9-inch springform pan. Bake at 450°, 5 minutes.

Combine softened cream cheese, sugar, lemon juice and lemon rind, mixing until well blended. Add eggs, one at a time, mixing well after each addition. Pour into the crust. Bake at 450°, 10 minutes. Reduce oven temperature to 300°; continue baking 30 minutes.

Combine sour cream, sugar and vanilla. Carefully spread over cheesecake. Continue baking 10 minutes. Loosen cake from rim of pan; cool before removing rim of pan. Chill. Top with fruit before serving.

Shortcake Supreme

2 cups flour
2 tablespoons sugar
1 tablespoon baking powder
½ teaspoon salt
1 egg, slightly beaten
⅔ cup milk
½ cup Parkay margarine, melted

*   *   *

1 cup Kraft marshmallow creme
1 cup heavy cream, whipped
1 teaspoon vanilla
1½ cups peach slices
1½ cups strawberry slices
½ cup blueberries

Combine dry ingredients. Add combined egg, milk and margarine, mixing just until moistened. Spread into greased and floured 8-inch layer pan. Bake at 450°, 12 to 15 minutes or until golden brown. Cool 10 minutes; remove from pan. Cool.

Combine marshmallow creme, 2 tablespoons heavy cream and vanilla; mix until well blended. Whip remaining heavy cream until stiff. Fold in marshmallow creme mixture. Split shortcake in half horizontally; fill with half of fruit and marshmallow creme mixture. Top with remaining fruit and marshmallow creme mixture.

8 to 10 servings

Whipping Cream

- Heavy cream has a fat content of at least 36%. It is also referred to as "whipping cream" and is generally used for whipping.
- Since cream doubles in volume when whipped, select a bowl of sufficient capacity.
- Cream, bowl and beaters should be thoroughly chilled before whipping.
- Beat until cream holds stiff peaks. Be careful not to overbeat or cream will separate.

Festive Fantasy Fudge

3 cups sugar
¾ cup Parkay margarine
⅔ cup (5⅓-fl. oz. can)
  evaporated milk
1 12-oz. pkg. semi-sweet
  chocolate pieces

1 7-oz. jar Kraft marshmallow
  creme
½ cup slivered almonds,
  toasted
1 3½-oz. can flaked
  coconut
1 teaspoon vanilla

Combine sugar, margarine and milk in heavy 2½-quart saucepan; bring to full rolling boil, stirring constantly. Continue boiling 5 minutes over medium heat, stirring constantly to prevent scorching. Remove from heat; stir in chocolate pieces until melted. Add remaining ingredients; beat until well blended. Pour into greased 13×9-inch baking pan. Cool at room temperature; cut into squares.

3 pounds

Spirited Bread Pudding

8 cups Italian bread cubes
1 cup raisins
5 eggs, slightly beaten
3 cups milk
1 cup sugar

¼ cup soft Parkay margarine,
  melted
1 tablespoon vanilla
  Bourbon Sauce

Place bread cubes and raisins in 11¾×7½-inch baking dish. Combine eggs, milk, sugar, margarine and vanilla; mix well. Pour over bread cubes. Let stand 10 minutes. Bake at 350°, 55 to 60 minutes or until firm. Cool slightly. Cut into squares; serve with:

Bourbon Sauce

1 cup sugar
1 egg

½ cup soft Parkay margarine
¼ cup bourbon

Combine ingredients in saucepan. Cook over low heat until sugar is dissolved, stirring constantly.

10 to 12 servings

Southern Pecan Tarts

14 Kraft caramels
2 tablespoons water
1 3⅛-oz. pkg. vanilla
    pudding and pie filling mix
1½ cups milk

    *   *   *

2 cups flour

½ teaspoon salt
⅔ cup Parkay margarine
4 to 6 tablespoons water

    *   *   *

25 Kraft caramels
¼ cup water
½ cup chopped pecans

Melt caramels with water in saucepan over low heat; stir frequently until smooth. Gradually add pudding mix and milk; cook, stirring constantly, until mixture comes to a boil. Chill.

Combine flour and salt; cut in margarine until mixture resembles coarse crumbs. Sprinkle with water while mixing lightly with a fork; form into a ball. Divide dough into twelve balls. On lightly floured surface, roll out each ball to 4½-inch circle. Place in 3-inch tart pans; prick with fork. Bake at 450°, 10 to 12 minutes or until golden brown. Cool. Spoon pudding mixture into shells. Chill.

Melt caramels with water in saucepan over low heat; stir frequently until smooth. Stir in nuts. Cool slightly. Spoon over tarts; chill.

Ribbon Fudge

3 cups sugar
¾ cup Parkay margarine
⅔ cup (5⅓-fl. oz. can)
    evaporated milk
1 6-oz. pkg. semi-sweet
    chocolate pieces

1 7-oz. jar Kraft marshmallow
    creme
1 teaspoon vanilla
½ cup peanut butter

Combine 1½ cups sugar, 6 tablespoons margarine and ⅓ cup milk in heavy 1½-quart saucepan; bring to full rolling boil, stirring constantly. Continue boiling 4 minutes over medium heat, stirring constantly to prevent scorching. Remove from heat; stir in chocolate pieces until melted. Add 1 cup marshmallow creme and ½ teaspoon vanilla; beat until well blended. Pour into greased 13×9-inch baking pan. Repeat procedure with remaining ingredients, substituting peanut butter for chocolate pieces. Spread over chocolate layer. Cool at room temperature; cut into squares.

3 pounds

Southern Pecan Tarts

Quick Dessert Ideas

- Combine ⅓ cup Parkay margarine, ¾ cup packed brown sugar, 3½-oz. can coconut and ½ cup chopped pecans. Spread on 13×9-inch yellow cake or slices of pound cake; broil until bubbly.
- Melt ⅓ cup Parkay margarine in chafing dish. Add ⅓ cup packed brown sugar; stir until sugar melts. Add peach, banana or pear slices; heat. Serve over ice cream.
- Cream ⅓ cup Parkay margarine. Blend in 1 teaspoon grated lemon or orange rind and dash of salt. Add 3 cups sifted confectioners' sugar alternately with 3 tablespoons lemon or orange juice; beat until fluffy. Frost a two-layer white, yellow or chocolate cake.
- Sauté apple slices in Parkay margarine. Sprinkle with cinnamon. Serve over ice cream.
- Cream ⅔ cup Parkay margarine; stir in ⅓ cup honey and 1 teaspoon grated orange rind. Serve with crêpes, waffles or Boston brown bread.

In The Beginning

This appealing selection of appetizers includes a variety of hot and cold specialties for casual gatherings, elegant entertaining and quick snacks. Enjoy such favorites as Cheddar Chips, Crab Puffs, Mushroom Appetizer Squares and Savory Party Mix.

Savory Party Mix

3 cups small pretzels
2 cups shoestring potatoes
2 cups Spanish peanuts
1½ cups seasoned croutons
½ cup (2 ozs.) Kraft grated
    parmesan cheese

1 3½-oz. can French fried
    onions
½ cup Squeeze Parkay
    margarine

Combine ingredients; mix lightly. Spread mixture on ungreased 15½×10½-inch jelly roll pan. Bake at 250°, 1 hour, stirring occasionally.

10 cups

Bacon-Onion Pinwheels

½ cup finely chopped onion
⅓ cup soft Parkay margarine
6 crisply cooked bacon slices,
    crumbled

2 tablespoons chopped parsley
2 8-oz. cans Pillsbury
    refrigerated quick
    Crescent dinner rolls

Combine onion, margarine, bacon and parsley; mix well. Separate dough into eight rectangles; firmly press perforations to seal. Spread margarine mixture over dough. Roll up each rectangle, starting at short end; cut into four slices. Place on ungreased cookie sheet, cut-side down; flatten slightly. Bake at 375°, 15 to 20 minutes or until golden brown.

Approximately 2½ dozen

Cheddar Chips

1 cup (4 ozs.) shredded Kraft
    sharp natural cheddar
    cheese
⅓ cup Parkay margarine
2 tablespoons milk

2 teaspoons Kraft pure
    prepared mustard
1 cup finely crushed potato
    chips
1 cup flour

Thoroughly blend cheese, margarine, milk and mustard. Add combined potato chips and flour; mix well. Shape dough into 10-inch roll. Wrap securely; chill overnight. Cut roll into ¼-inch slices; place on ungreased cookie sheet. Bake at 375°, 10 to 12 minutes or until edges are lightly browned.

Approximately 2½ dozen

Savory Party Mix, Bacon-Onion Pinwheels

Shrimp Sauté

½ cup soft Parkay margarine
1 teaspoon basil leaves,
  crushed
½ teaspoon salt
4½ cups (1½ lbs.) cleaned
  cooked shrimp

1 16-oz. can small whole
  onions, drained
2 green peppers, cut into
  squares
½ lb. mushroom caps
¼ cup dry white wine

Melt margarine; stir in remaining ingredients. Cook 5 to 10 minutes or until vegetables are crisp-tender. Keep warm; serve with picks.

Contemporary Appetizer Puffs

1 cup Parkay margarine
1½ cups flour
½ cup dairy sour cream
  Chopped green onion
  Chopped mushrooms

Chopped pitted ripe
  olives
Kraft grated
  parmesan cheese

Cut margarine into flour until mixture begins to form a ball. Blend in sour cream. Divide dough into quarters. Wrap securely; chill several hours. On floured surface, roll out each quarter to 12×6-inch rectangle. Sprinkle one half of each rectangle with green onion, mushroom, olives or cheese. Fold dough over filling to form 6-inch square. Cut into 2-inch squares; cut each square in half diagonally. Lightly press edges together. Place on ungreased cookie sheet. Bake at 350°, 15 to 18 minutes or until lightly browned. Serve hot.

6 dozen

Variation: Fold dough over filling to form 6-inch square. Cut into 2-inch squares; lightly press edges together. Place on ungreased cookie sheet. Bake at 350°, 15 to 18 minutes.

Hot Mulled Punch

½ cup granulated sugar
½ cup packed brown sugar
½ teaspoon ground allspice
¼ teaspoon ground cloves
6 cups apple cider

2 qts. Kraft pure 100%
unsweetened pasteurized
orange juice
Soft Parkay margarine
Cinnamon sticks

Combine sugars and spices. Add cider; heat, stirring until sugar is dissolved. Bring to boil; simmer 5 minutes. Add orange juice; heat thoroughly. Top each serving with 1 tablespoon margarine; stir with cinnamon stick.

Fifteen 1-cup servings

Tropical Appetizer Dip

¼ cup chopped green pepper
¼ cup Parkay margarine
1 lb. Velveeta pasteurized
process cheese spread,
cubed

1 8¼-oz. can crushed
pineapple, undrained
¼ cup slivered almonds,
toasted
French bread chunks

Sauté green pepper in margarine in fondue pot or saucepan. Add process cheese spread, pineapple and nuts; heat until process cheese spread is melted, stirring occasionally. Serve warm with bread.

3 cups

Liptauer Spread

1 8-oz. pkg. Philadelphia
Brand cream cheese
½ cup soft Parkay margarine
2 tablespoons finely chopped
onion
1½ teaspoons anchovy paste

1 teaspoon Kraft pure
prepared mustard
1 teaspoon capers, chopped
1 teaspoon caraway seed
1 teaspoon paprika

Combine softened cream cheese and margarine, mixing until well blended. Add remaining ingredients; mix well. Chill. Serve with French or pumpernickel bread.

1½ cups

Crab Puffs

1 7½-oz. can (1½ cups)
   crabmeat, drained, flaked
½ cup chopped green pepper
½ cup chopped celery
⅓ cup chopped pitted ripe
   olives

Dash of hot pepper sauce
Kraft real mayonnaise
Miniature Cream Puffs

Combine crabmeat, green pepper, celery, olives, hot pepper sauce and enough mayonnaise to moisten; mix lightly. Cut tops from Miniature Cream Puffs; fill with crabmeat mixture. Replace tops.

Miniature Cream Puffs

½ cup water
¼ cup Parkay margarine
½ cup flour

Dash of salt
2 eggs

Bring water and margarine to boil. Add flour and salt; stir vigorously over low heat until mixture forms a ball. Remove from heat. Add eggs, one at a time, beating well after each addition. Drop rounded teaspoonfuls of batter onto ungreased cookie sheet. Bake at 400°, 30 to 35 minutes or until golden brown. Remove from cookie sheet immediately; cool.

2½ dozen

Mushroom Appetizer Squares

1 8-oz. can Pillsbury
   refrigerated quick Crescent
   dinner rolls
2 cups mushroom slices
¼ cup Parkay margarine, melted

½ cup (2 ozs.) shredded
   Casino brand natural
   monterey jack cheese
½ teaspoon oregano leaves,
   crushed
¼ teaspoon onion salt

Separate dough into two long rectangles. Press onto bottom and ½ inch high around sides of 13×9-inch baking pan. Toss mushrooms with margarine; arrange on dough. Sprinkle with cheese and seasonings. Bake at 375°, 20 to 25 minutes. Cut into squares. Serve warm.

2 dozen

Salami Spread

1 3-oz. pkg. Philadelphia
   Brand cream cheese
½ cup Squeeze Parkay
   margarine

2 cups (8 ozs.) shredded
   Kraft sharp natural
   cheddar cheese
½ cup finely chopped salami

Combine softened cream cheese and margarine, mixing until well blended. Add cheddar cheese and salami; mix well. Serve with assorted crackers.

2 cups

Variations: Substitute finely chopped ham or cleaned cooked shrimp for salami.

Add 1 tablespoon finely chopped green onion or parsley.

Appetizer Quiche

1 cup flour
¼ teaspoon salt
⅓ cup Parkay margarine
3 to 4 tablespoons water
    *   *   *
2 eggs, slightly beaten
¾ cup milk
½ teaspoon salt
  Dash of pepper

1½ cups (6 ozs.) shredded
   Kraft aged natural
   Swiss cheese
1 tablespoon flour
1 4-oz. can mushrooms,
   drained, chopped
2 tablespoons chopped green
   onion

Combine flour and salt; cut in margarine until mixture resembles coarse crumbs. Sprinkle with water while mixing lightly with a fork; form into a ball. On lightly floured surface, roll out dough to 12-inch square. Place on bottom and 1 inch high around sides of 9-inch square pan.

Combine eggs, milk and seasonings; mix well. Toss cheese with flour; add with remaining ingredients to egg mixture. Pour into pastry shell. Bake at 325°, 45 to 50 minutes or until set. Let stand 10 minutes; cut into squares.

Approximately 2 dozen

Variation: Substitute shredded Kraft sharp cheddar cheese for Swiss cheese.

Tuna Tidbits

1 6½-oz. can tuna, drained,
  flaked
1 5-oz. jar Old English sharp
  pasteurized process cheese
  spread
½ cup soft Parkay margarine

2 tablespoons chopped pimiento
2 tablespoons finely chopped
  green pepper
6 English muffins, split,
  toasted

Combine tuna, process cheese spread, margarine, pimiento and green pepper; mix well. Spread on muffin halves; broil until spread is hot and bubbly. Cut into quarters.

4 dozen

Savory Stuffed Mushooms

1 lb. fresh mushrooms
⅔ cup soft bread crumbs
¼ cup Squeeze Parkay margarine

1 teaspoon chopped green
  onion
¼ teaspoon garlic salt

Remove mushroom stems; chop stems. Combine stems and remaining ingredients; mix well. Fill mushroom caps; place on rack of broiler pan. Broil 2 to 3 minutes or until golden brown. Serve hot.

2½ to 3 dozen

Curried Party Mix

½ cup Squeeze Parkay
  margarine
1 teaspoon curry powder
¼ teaspoon ginger
2 cups bite-size crispy rice
  squares

2 cups bite-size crispy
  wheat squares
2 cups raisins
2 cups pretzel sticks
2 cups peanuts or walnut
  halves

Combine margarine and seasonings. Pour over combined remaining ingredients; mix lightly. Spread mixture on ungreased 15½×10½-inch jelly roll pan. Bake at 250°, 1 hour, stirring occasionally.

Approximately 10 cups

Beignets

1 cup water	2 cups (8 ozs.) shredded
¼ cup Parkay margarine	Cracker Barrel brand sharp
1 cup flour	natural cheddar cheese
½ teaspoon salt	Oil
3 eggs	

Bring water and margarine to boil. Add flour and salt; stir vigorously over low heat until mixture forms a ball. Remove from heat. Add eggs, one at a time, beating well after each addition. Stir in cheese. Drop rounded teaspoonfuls of batter into deep hot oil, 350°. Fry until golden brown, turning once. Drain.

4½ to 5 dozen

Italian Fondue

1 chicken bouillon cube	2 cups (8 ozs.) shredded
1 cup boiling water	Kraft natural low
¼ cup Parkay margarine	moisture part-skim
¼ cup flour	mozzarella cheese
½ cup milk	Cauliflowerets
1 tablespoon green	Broccoli pieces,
onion slices	partially cooked
	Red pepper strips
	Bread sticks

Dissolve bouillon in boiling water. Make a white sauce with margarine, flour, milk and bouillon. Stir in onions. Add ½ cup cheese; stir constantly until melted. Repeat until all cheese has been added. Keep dip hot while serving. Serve with vegetables and bread sticks.

2¼ cups

Dill Wafers

½ cup Parkay margarine	1 cup flour
1 3-oz. pkg. Philadelphia Brand	1 teaspoon dill weed
cream cheese	

Combine margarine and softened cream cheese, mixing until well blended. Add flour and dill weed; mix well. Chill. On lightly floured surface, roll out dough to ⅛-inch thickness. Cut with assorted 1½-inch cutters; place on ungreased cookie sheet. Bake at 425°, 8 to 10 minutes or until lightly browned.

Approximately 4 dozen

Crunchy Parmesan Popcorn

10 to 12 cups hot unsalted
   popped corn
⅓ cup Squeeze Parkay
   margarine

⅓ cup Kraft grated parmesan
   cheese

Combine ingredients; toss lightly until well coated. Spread single layer of mixture on ungreased 15½×10½-inch jelly roll pan. Bake at 375°, 6 to 8 minutes or until golden brown.

10 to 12 cups

Festive Cheddar Spritz

3 cups (12 ozs.) shredded
   Kraft sharp natural
   cheddar cheese
½ cup Parkay margarine

2 tablespoons milk
1⅔ cups flour
½ teaspoon salt
¼ teaspoon dry mustard

Thoroughly blend cheese, margarine and milk. Add combined dry ingredients; mix well. Force dough through cookie press onto ungreased cookie sheet. Bake at 375°, 10 to 12 minutes or until edges are golden brown.

Approximately 7 dozen

Variation: Substitute whole-wheat flour for ⅔ cup all-purpose
   flour.

Herb Shrimp Canapes

1 4½-oz. can shrimp,
   rinsed, drained, chopped
¼ cup soft Parkay margarine
1 teaspoon lemon juice
¼ teaspoon dill weed

⅛ teaspoon hot pepper sauce
Cucumber slices, ¼-inch
   thick
Party rye bread slices

Combine shrimp, margarine, lemon juice, dill weed and hot pepper sauce; mix lightly. Spread on cucumber or bread slices.

¾ cup

Quick Appetizers

• Heat tomato juice with a dash or two of hot pepper sauce; top with a dollop of soft Parkay margarine.

• Brush grapefruit halves with melted Parkay margarine; sprinkle with ground ginger or cinnamon. Broil until bubbly.

• Combine ¼ cup Squeeze Parkay margarine, 4 cups pecans or walnuts, 1 teaspoon salt and 1 teaspoon curry powder. Bake at 350°, 10 to 12 minutes, stirring occasionally.

• Toss popped corn with Squeeze Parkay margarine and crushed oregano leaves, onion salt or garlic salt.

• Remove stems from 1 lb. mushrooms. Combine chopped mushroom stems, ½ cup Kraft grated parmesan cheese, ¼ cup Squeeze Parkay margarine and 1 tablespoon chopped onion. Refill mushroom caps; broil until hot.

• Combine ½ cup soft Parkay margarine, ¼ cup crisply cooked crumbled bacon, ¼ cup chopped tomato and ⅛ teaspoon dill seed. Spread on toasted English muffins or bread slices; cut into quarters.

Side By Side

Main dish accompaniments are too often neglected in meal planning. With a little fore-thought and a few intriguing recipes, side dishes can add new interest to everyday meals and guest dinners. Fried Rice, Herbed Tomatoes and Potatoes Elégante are just a few of our suggestions to stimulate your imagination.

Potato Pancakes

1 egg, beaten
2 tablespoons flour
2 tablespoons grated onion
¼ teaspoon salt

2 cups shredded potatoes,
 rinsed, drained
½ cup Squeeze Parkay
 margarine

Combine egg, flour, onion and salt; mix well. Stir in potatoes. Heat margarine in skillet. For each pancake, fry ¼ cup mixture until crisp and golden brown on both sides.

6 to 8 servings

Baked Fruit Compote

½ cup pitted prunes
1 20-oz. can pineapple slices,
 drained, cut in half
1 16-oz. can pear halves,
 drained, cut in half
1 16-oz. can apricot halves,
 drained

¼ cup Squeeze Parkay
 margarine
¼ cup packed brown sugar
1 teaspoon ginger
¼ teaspoon cinnamon
1 tablespoon brandy

Place prunes in 1-quart casserole. Cover with combined pineapple, pears and apricots. Spoon combined margarine, sugar and spices over fruit. Cover; bake at 350°, 25 minutes or until hot and bubbly. Add brandy; mix lightly.

6 to 8 servings

Croutons

2 cups bread cubes

¼ cup Squeeze Parkay
 margarine

Toss bread cubes with margarine. Place on ungreased baking pan. Bake at 400°, 8 to 10 minutes or until lightly browned, stirring occasionally. Sprinkle on soups or salads.

1 cup

Variations: For extra flavor, add ¼ teaspoon oregano or basil leaves, onion salt, garlic powder or Italian seasoning before baking.

Vegetable Stuffed Acorn Squash

2 acorn squash, halved, seeded
1 cup broccoli flowerets
1 cup mushroom slices
¾ cup celery slices
½ cup carrot slices
½ cup coarsely chopped onion
½ cup Parkay margarine
½ teaspoon oregano leaves, crushed
½ teaspoon salt
Dash of pepper
¼ cup slivered almonds

Place squash in baking dish, cut-side down. Bake at 400°, 40 minutes. Sauté remaining vegetables in margarine until crisp-tender. Stir in seasonings. Fill centers of squash with vegetable mixture; sprinkle with nuts. Continue baking 15 to 20 minutes or until squash is tender.

4 servings

Calico Corn

1 cup celery slices
¼ cup Parkay margarine
1 17-oz. can whole kernel corn, drained
¼ cup chopped green pepper
2 tablespoons chopped onion
2 tablespoons chopped pimiento

Sauté celery in margarine until tender. Add remaining ingredients; heat.

6 servings

Sour Creamed Beans

1 onion, thinly sliced
Parkay margarine
2 10-oz. pkgs. frozen green beans, thawed, drained
1 cup dairy sour cream
¼ cup flour
1½ teaspoons salt
¼ teaspoon pepper
1 cup (4 ozs.) shredded Kraft sharp natural cheddar cheese
1 cup soft bread crumbs

Sauté onion in ¼ cup margarine. Add to combined beans, sour cream, flour and seasonings; mix lightly. Pour into greased 1½-quart casserole. Sprinkle with cheese; top with crumbs tossed with ¼ cup melted margarine. Bake at 350°, 25 minutes.

4 to 6 servings

Herb Sauced Artichokes

6 medium artichokes	Lemon Herb Sauce
Piquant Sauce	Caper Sauce

Rinse whole artichokes in cold water. Cut 1 inch from top; cut off stem and tips of leaves. Place in boiling, salted water. Cover; cook 35 to 45 minutes or until leaves can be removed easily. Drain. Serve with any of the following sauces:

Piquant Sauce

½ cup Parkay margarine	1 teaspoon salt
1 egg, beaten	1 teaspoon sugar
2 tablespoons vinegar	½ teaspoon marjoram leaves
1 tablespoon lemon juice	1 garlic clove, minced

Melt margarine in saucepan over low heat. Blend in remaining ingredients. Cook, stirring constantly, until thickened.

Lemon Herb Sauce

½ cup Parkay margarine	½ teaspoon dry mustard
2 tablespoons lemon juice	Dash of salt and pepper
½ teaspoon basil leaves	

Melt margarine. Stir in remaining ingredients; heat thoroughly.

Caper Sauce

½ cup Parkay margarine	1 teaspoon chopped capers
1 tablespoon lemon juice	
1 teaspoon Kraft horseradish sauce	

Melt margarine. Stir in remaining ingredients; heat thoroughly.

6 servings

To eat an artichoke, draw the tender part of the leaves between your teeth. Remove the prickly choke and eat the delicate heart with a fork.

Caraway Carrots

12 medium carrots, cut into
   quarters
¼ cup Parkay margarine
2 tablespoons chopped parsley

1 teaspoon caraway seed
¼ teaspoon salt
Dash of pepper

Cook carrots in boiling water until crisp-tender; drain. Add remaining ingredients; mix lightly.

8 servings

Twice Baked Potatoes

4 large baked potatoes
1½ cups (6 ozs.) shredded Kraft
   sharp natural cheddar
   cheese
2 tablespoons milk
¼ cup Parkay margarine

½ teaspoon salt
Dash of pepper
2 tablespoons chopped chives
4 crisply cooked bacon
   slices, crumbled

Slice potatoes in half lengthwise. Scoop out centers, leaving ⅛-inch shell. Mash potatoes. Add 1 cup cheese, milk, margarine and seasonings; beat until fluffy. If too dry, beat in additional milk as required. Stir in 1 tablespoon chives and half of bacon; fill shells. Bake at 350°, 20 minutes. Combine remaining cheese, chives and bacon; sprinkle over potatoes. Continue baking 10 minutes.

8 servings

Company Peas

1 10-oz. pkg. frozen peas,
   cooked, drained
¼ cup soft Parkay margarine

1 cup shredded lettuce
1 tablespoon chopped parsley

Combine peas and margarine; heat. Add remaining ingredients; toss lightly. Serve immediately.

4 servings

Vegetables Sicily

3 cups zucchini slices
1 medium onion, sliced
1 teaspoon oregano leaves,
    crushed
½ teaspoon salt

¼ teaspoon pepper
⅓ cup Parkay margarine
1 medium tomato, cut into
    wedges

Sauté zucchini, onion and seasonings in margarine. Add tomato; cook 5 minutes or until vegetables are tender.

4 to 6 servings

Herb Bread

½ cup Squeeze Parkay
    margarine
½ teaspoon thyme
½ teaspoon basil leaves,
    crushed

⅛ teaspoon onion salt
    Italian or French bread,
    cut into 1-inch slices

Combine margarine and seasonings; mix well. Spread one side of each bread slice with margarine mixture. Place on ungreased cookie sheet; spread-side up. Bake at 425°, 10 to 12 minutes or until golden brown.

Parmesan Herb Bread

½ cup soft Parkay margarine
¼ cup (1 oz.) Kraft grated
    parmesan cheese
½ teaspoon oregano leaves,
    crushed

¼ teaspoon basil leaves,
    crushed
⅛ teaspoon garlic salt
1 Vienna bread loaf, sliced

Combine margarine, cheese and seasonings; mix well. Spread one side of each bread slice with margarine mixture. Place on ungreased cookie sheet, spread-side up. Bake at 400°, 12 to 15 minutes or until golden brown.

Variation: Substitute ⅓ cup crushed French fried onions for cheese and seasonings.

Calico Bread

1 1½-lb. round Italian
bread loaf
¾ cup soft Parkay margarine

3 tablespoons finely chopped
sweet cherry peppers
1 teaspoon oregano leaves,
crushed

Cut bread into twelve wedges. Combine margarine, peppers and oregano; mix well. Spread both sides of each wedge with margarine mixture. Reassemble loaf; wrap in aluminum foil. Bake at 400°, 25 minutes.

To Make Ahead: Prepare as directed. Wrap securely in aluminum foil; refrigerate. When ready to serve, bake at 400°, 35 minutes.

Variation: Substitute Vienna or French bread for Italian bread.

Rice Shoyu

1 cup rice
3 tablespoons sesame seed,
toasted
¼ cup Parkay margarine
1½ cups water
¼ cup soy sauce

6 green onions, cut into
1-inch pieces
1 16-oz. can bean sprouts,
drained
1 cup mushroom slices

Stir-fry rice and sesame seed in margarine until brown. Add water and soy sauce; bring to boil. Cover; simmer 20 minutes. Add remaining ingredients. Cover; simmer additional 5 minutes or until vegetables are tender.

6 servings

This far eastern rice dish is a delicious complement to midwestern baked ham, broiled chicken or roast pork.

Grilled Parmesan Corn

½ cup (2 ozs.) Kraft grated
  parmesan cheese
½ cup soft Parkay margarine

1 tablespoon chopped parsley
½ teaspoon salt
8 ears corn

Combine cheese, margarine, parsley and salt; mix well. Spread rounded tablespoonful of mixture on each ear of corn; wrap securely in aluminum foil. Place on grill over medium-low coals. Cook 20 to 30 minutes or until corn is done.

8 servings

Stir-Fried Broccoli 'N Cheese

2 10-oz. pkgs. frozen chopped
  broccoli, thawed,
  well-drained
½ cup (2 ozs.) Kraft grated
  parmesan cheese

⅓ cup chopped onion
½ teaspoon salt
⅓ cup Squeeze Parkay
  margarine

Sauté combined broccoli, cheese, onion and salt in margarine until lightly browned, stirring occasionally. Top with additional cheese, if desired.

4 to 6 servings

Fried Rice

1½ cups celery slices
¼ cup chopped onion
¼ cup Squeeze Parkay
  margarine

2 cups cooked rice
2 eggs, beaten
1 tablespoon soy sauce

Sauté celery and onion in margarine. Add rice; cook over low heat 2 to 3 minutes, stirring occasionally. Add eggs and soy sauce; continue cooking until eggs are cooked, stirring occasionally.

4 to 6 servings

Potatoes Elégante

6 medium potatoes, peeled,
thinly sliced
⅓ cup Squeeze Parkay
margarine

1 cup (4 ozs.) Kraft grated
parmesan cheese

Rinse potato slices thoroughly; dry. Brush 1 tablespoon margarine onto bottom and sides of 9-inch pie plate; sprinkle with 1 tablespoon cheese. Toss potatoes with remaining margarine. Layer half of potatoes on bottom and sides of pie plate; sprinkle with cheese. Repeat layers. Bake at 400°, 1 hour or until potatoes are tender. Invert onto serving plate immediately.

4 to 6 servings

Eggplant Parmigiana

2 medium eggplant,
peeled, cut into
½-inch slices
Parkay margarine
1 15½-oz. jar
spaghetti sauce

½ cup (2 ozs.) Kraft grated
parmesan cheese
1 4-oz. pkg. Kraft shredded
natural low moisture
part-skim mozzarella
cheese

Sauté eggplant in margarine until tender, adding margarine as needed. In 10×6-inch baking dish, layer half of eggplant, sauce and cheeses; repeat layers. Bake at 350°, 25 minutes.

6 servings

Eggplant, tomatoes and parmesan cheese — a delicious combination and very Italian! For a meatless supper, serve with hot Italian bread and a tossed green salad. For a heartier dinner, complete the meal with broiled chicken, roast beef or baked fish fillets.

Oven-Fried Potatoes

3 medium potatoes, unpeeled,   1½ teaspoons salt
    cut into lengthwise strips   1 teaspoon dill weed
⅓ cup Squeeze Parkay
    margarine

Rinse potatoes thoroughly; dry. Combine potatoes, margarine and seasonings; toss lightly. Spread potatoes on 15½×10½-inch jelly roll pan. Bake at 450°, 40 minutes stirring once.

4 to 6 servings

Tempting Long Loaf

¼ cup chopped onion   1 tablespoon chopped pimiento
¼ cup chopped green pepper   1 Italian bread loaf
½ cup soft Parkay margarine
1 cup (4 ozs.) Kraft shredded
    natural low moisture
    part-skim mozzarella
    cheese

Sauté onion and green pepper in 1 tablespoon margarine. Add remaining margarine, cheese and pimiento; mix well. Cut bread in half lengthwise; cut each half crosswise into 1½-inch slices within ½ inch of bottom crust. Spread with margarine mixture; wrap each half in aluminum foil. Bake at 375°, 15 minutes.

Sautéed Parmesan Rice

½ cup green onion slices   ¼ cup chopped parsley
½ cup Squeeze Parkay   ½ cup (2 ozs.) Kraft grated
    margarine   parmesan cheese
4 cups cooked rice
2 6-oz. cans water chestnuts,
    drained, sliced

Sauté onion in margarine. Add rice, water chestnuts and parsley; cook over low heat until rice is lightly browned. Stir in cheese.

8 servings

Herbed Tomatoes

4 medium tomatoes
Salt
2 cups soft bread crumbs
¼ cup chopped
parsley
¼ cup soft Parkay margarine

2 teaspoons Dijon-style
mustard
½ teaspoon basil leaves
¼ teaspoon tarragon leaves
¼ cup (1 oz.) Kraft shredded
natural Swiss cheese

Cut off tops of tomatoes. Remove pulp, leaving ¼-inch shell. Lightly sprinkle inside of tomatoes with salt; drain on absorbent paper. Combine crumbs, parsley, margarine and mustard in skillet; cook over low heat 3 to 5 minutes or until crumbs are lightly browned, stirring frequently. Stir in seasonings. Place tomatoes in 10×6-inch baking dish; fill with crumb mixture. Sprinkle with cheese. Loosely cover; bake at 375°, 20 minutes.

4 servings

Curried Vegetables

¼ cup Squeeze Parkay
margarine
1 teaspoon curry powder

1 10-oz. pkg. frozen peas,
cooked, drained
1 cup chopped cooked potatoes
Salt and pepper

Combine margarine and curry. Add vegetables; heat. Season to taste.

4 servings

Country Carrots and Zucchini

4 6-inch zucchini
1 cup chopped cooked carrots
½ cup soft bread crumbs
3 tablespoons Kraft grated
parmesan cheese
3 tablespoons Squeeze Parkay
margarine

⅛ teaspoon marjoram leaves
Dash of pepper
Salt
1 tablespoon chopped
parsley

Cook zucchini in boiling water until tender; drain. Cut zucchini in half lengthwise. Scoop out centers, leaving ¼-inch shell; drain. Chop zucchini removed from center. Add carrots, crumbs, cheese, margarine, marjoram and pepper; mix lightly. Sprinkle zucchini shells with salt; fill with vegetable mixture. Sprinkle with parsley. Place in shallow baking dish. Bake at 350°, 15 minutes.

8 servings

Easy Accompaniments

- Combine ½ cup soft Parkay margarine, ¼ cup honey and 2 teaspoons cinnamon. Toss with cooked carrots or spoon into baked acorn squash.

- Combine ½ cup soft Parkay margarine, ¼ cup Kraft grated parmesan cheese and 1 tablespoon chopped chives. Use on baked potatoes or cooked vegetables.

- Combine ½ cup Squeeze Parkay margarine, 1 tablespoon lemon juice and 1 tablespoon chopped parsley. Use as a sauce for hot vegetables.

- Combine ½ cup soft Parkay margarine, 2 tablespoons mustard and dash of cayenne. Use on hot cooked green beans, broccoli, asparagus or cauliflower.

- Sauté fresh vegetables such as mushrooms or onions in Squeeze Parkay margarine.

- Toss hot cooked rice, noodles or pasta with Squeeze Parkay margarine and Kraft grated parmesan cheese.

Sauced, Spiced And Special

Savory casseroles, oven-baked chicken, grilled sandwiches and festive crêpes are just a few of the imaginative main dish recipes which have been developed to please even the most discerning gourmet.

Crunchy Parmesan Chicken

¾ cup (3 ozs.) Kraft grated
   parmesan cheese
1 3-oz. can French fried
   onions, crushed
¼ cup dry bread crumbs
1 teaspoon paprika
½ teaspoon salt

Dash of pepper
1 2½ to 3-lb.
   broiler-fryer, cut up
1 egg, slightly beaten
1 tablespoon milk
¼ cup Parkay margarine,
   melted

Combine cheese, onion, crumbs and seasonings. Dip chicken in combined egg and milk; coat with cheese mixture. Place in 11¾×7½-inch baking dish; pour margarine over chicken. Bake at 350°, 55 to 60 minutes or until tender.

3 to 4 servings

A crispy favorite for indoor or outdoor dining. Tote to picnics in a well-insulated carrier.

Chicken 'N Lemon

1 2½ to 3-lb. broiler-
   fryer, cut up
½ cup flour
1 teaspoon grated lemon rind
1½ teaspoons salt
½ teaspoon paprika

½ teaspoon pepper
⅓ cup Parkay margarine,
   melted
¼ cup lemon juice
2 tablespoons chopped parsley

Coat chicken with combined flour, lemon rind and seasonings. Place in 11¾×7½-inch baking dish. Pour combined margarine and lemon juice over chicken. Bake at 375°, 1 hour or until tender. Sprinkle with parsley. Garnish with lemon slices, if desired.

3 to 4 servings

Double or triple the recipe for a crowd and serve with hot rice, crescent rolls and a tossed fruit salad.

Golden Oven-Fried Chicken

2 2½ to 3-lb. broiler-
 fryers, cut up
2 eggs, slightly beaten
2 tablespoons milk
1½ cups dry bread crumbs

2 teaspoons salt
1 teaspoon paprika
Dash of pepper
Squeeze Parkay margarine

Dip chicken in combined eggs and milk; coat with combined crumbs and seasonings. Place in 15½×10½-inch jelly roll pan; pour margarine over chicken. Bake at 375°, 1 hour or until tender.

8 servings

Crispy Sesame Chicken

1 2½ to 3-lb. broiler-
 fryer, cut up
1 egg, slightly beaten
½ cup milk
½ cup flour

¼ cup sesame seed, toasted
2 teaspoons salt
Dash of pepper
Squeeze Parkay margarine

Dip chicken in combined egg and milk; coat with combined flour and seasonings. Repeat. Place in 13½×8¾-inch baking dish. Pour margarine over chicken. Bake at 375°, 1 hour or until tender.

3 to 4 servings

Creamy Brunch Eggs

¼ cup Parkay margarine
¼ cup flour
2 cups milk
½ teaspoon salt
 Dash of pepper
1 cup (4 ozs.) shredded Kraft
 sharp natural cheddar
 cheese

8 hard-cooked eggs, sliced
1 4-oz. can mushrooms,
 drained
¼ cup green onion slices
2 tablespoons chopped
 pimiento
4 English muffins, split,
 toasted

Make a white sauce with margarine, flour, milk and seasonings. Add cheese; stir until melted. Add eggs, mushrooms, onion and pimiento; heat thoroughly. Serve over muffins.

8 servings

Country Cornish Hens

½ lb. bulk pork sausage
2 cups bread cubes, toasted
1 cup chopped peeled apples
½ cup celery slices
⅓ cup raisins
⅓ cup chopped onion
¾ cup Parkay margarine, melted

⅓ cup sherry
¼ teaspoon sage
¼ teaspoon salt
Dash of pepper
6 1 to 1½-lb. Rock Cornish hens

Brown meat; drain. Add bread, apples, celery, raisins, onion, ¼ cup margarine, 2 tablespoons sherry and seasonings; mix well. Lightly stuff hens with dressing mixture; close openings with skewers. Bake at 400°, 1 hour or until tender, basting occasionally with combined remaining margarine and sherry. Garnish with celery leaves, if desired.

6 servings

Chicken Mushroom Crêpes

2 eggs, slightly beaten
½ cup flour
½ teaspoon salt
½ cup milk
1 tablespoon Squeeze Parkay margarine

* * *

½ cup chopped celery
¼ cup Squeeze Parkay margarine

¼ cup flour
¾ cup chicken broth
¾ cup milk
½ cup dry white wine
½ cup (2 ozs.) shredded Kraft natural Swiss cheese
2 cups chopped cooked chicken
1 4-oz. can mushrooms, drained

Combine eggs, flour, salt, milk and margarine; beat until smooth. Let stand 30 minutes. For each crêpe, pour ¼ cup batter into hot, lightly greased 8-inch skillet. Cook on one side only until underside is lightly browned.

Sauté celery in margarine. Blend in flour. Gradually add combined broth, milk and wine; cook over low heat, stirring constantly, until thickened. Add cheese; stir until melted. Stir in chicken and mushrooms. Fill each crêpe with ⅓ cup chicken mixture; roll up. Place in 11¾×7½-inch baking dish, seam-side down. Top with remaining chicken mixture. Bake at 350°, 20 minutes.

4 servings

Chelsea Ham Casserole

¾ cup Squeeze Parkay
½ cup flour
2½ cups milk
1 teaspoon salt
2 10-oz. pkgs. frozen chopped
    broccoli, cooked, drained

2 cups chopped ham
⅓ cup slivered almonds,
    toasted
2 cups soft bread crumbs

Make a white sauce with ½ cup margarine, flour, milk and salt. Stir in broccoli, ham and nuts. Spoon into 2-quart casserole. Top with crumbs tossed with remaining margarine. Bake at 350°, 25 minutes.

6 to 8 servings

Variations: Substitute cooked chicken or pork for ham.

Substitute sliced water chestnuts for almonds.

Polynesian Crêpes

3 eggs, slightly beaten
¾ cup flour
½ teaspoon salt
1 cup milk
1 tablespoon oil
      *   *   *
1 20-oz. can crushed pineapple
½ cup soft Parkay margarine

¼ cup packed brown sugar
1 teaspoon ginger
2 cups finely chopped ham
1½ cups cooked rice
⅓ cup chopped green pepper
1 tablespoon cornstarch
⅓ cup water

Combine eggs, flour, salt, milk and oil; beat until smooth. Let stand 30 minutes. For each crêpe, pour 2 tablespoons batter into hot, lightly greased 8-inch skillet. Cook on one side only until underside is browned.

Drain pineapple, reserving ¾ cup syrup. Combine margarine, sugar and ginger. Add pineapple, ham, rice and green pepper; mix well. Fill each crêpe with ⅓ cup ham mixture; roll up. Place in 15½×10½-inch jelly roll pan, seam-side down. Bake at 375°, 20 minutes. Gradually add reserved syrup to cornstarch, stirring until well blended. Gradually add water; bring to boil. Boil 3 minutes, stirring constantly, until mixture clears and thickens. Serve with crêpes.

8 servings

Pork Pilaf

1½ lbs. pork, cut into 1-inch
    cubes
⅓ cup Squeeze Parkay
    margarine
1 cup chopped onion
½ cup chopped green pepper
1 beef bouillon cube

1½ cups boiling water
1 16-oz. can tomatoes
1 cup rice
½ cup raisins
1 teaspoon salt
½ teaspoon cinnamon
½ teaspoon curry powder

Brown meat in margarine in large skillet. Add onion and green pepper; cook until tender. Dissolve bouillon cube in boiling water; add to meat mixture with remaining ingredients. Cover; simmer 30 to 35 minutes or until meat is tender.

4 to 6 servings

Variation: Omit raisins. Add 1 cup chopped apple during last 10
    minutes of cooking.

Linguine Carbonara

2 cups broccoli flowerets
1½ cups mushroom slices
½ cup Parkay margarine
⅓ cup flour
    Dash of pepper
2½ cups milk

¼ cup (1 oz.) Kraft grated
    parmesan cheese
4 crisply cooked bacon
    slices, crumbled
8 ozs. linguine, cooked,
    drained

Sauté broccoli and mushrooms in margarine. Blend in flour and pepper. Gradually add milk; cook, stirring constantly, until thickened. Add cheese and bacon; stir until cheese is melted. Combine with linguine; toss lightly.

4 to 6 servings

Stuffin' Topped Halibut

2 cups soft bread crumbs	¼ teaspoon sage
½ cup Squeeze Parkay margarine	¼ teaspoon salt
½ cup chopped celery	4 frozen halibut steaks,
¼ cup chopped onion	¾-inch thick

Combine crumbs, margarine, celery, onion and seasonings; mix well. Place fish in 11¾×7½-inch baking dish; top with crumb mixture. Bake at 350°, 30 to 35 minutes or until crumb mixture is golden brown and fish flakes easily with fork.

4 servings

Variations: Substitute salmon steaks for halibut.

Substitute dill weed for sage.

Fettucine Magnifico

½ cup Parkay margarine	½ cup (2 ozs.) Kraft grated
⅓ cup flour	parmesan cheese
2 cups half and half	8 ozs. fettucine noodles,
¼ teaspoon garlic salt	cooked, drained
Dash of pepper	

Make a white sauce with margarine, flour, half and half and seasonings. Add cheese; stir until melted. Combine with noodles; toss lightly.

4 to 6 servings

Variation: Add 1 cup chopped ham.

An American version of an Italian classic that can be served as a main dish or an accompaniment.

Stuffin' Topped Halibut, Caraway Carrots (page 113)

Baked Fish

1 3 to 4-lb. white fish, pan-dressed	Squeeze Parkay margarine Lemon Chive Sauce

Place fish in large well-greased baking dish. Generously brush inside and outside with margarine. Bake at 350°, 45 to 50 minutes or until fish flakes easily with fork. Serve with:

Lemon Chive Sauce

½ cup Squeeze Parkay margarine 3 tablespoons lemon juice	1 tablespoon chopped chives 2 teaspoons grated lemon rind

Combine ingredients; mix well. Serve hot or cold.

4 to 6 servings

Variation: Substitute green onion or parsley for chives.

For a touch of elegance, garnish fish with lemon twists and watercress.

Celtic Fish Fillets

2 lbs. fish fillets ½ cup milk 1 cup cornmeal	1½ teaspoons salt Squeeze Parkay margarine Celtic Egg Sauce

Dip fish in mix; coat with combined cornmeal and salt. Fry in margarine until golden brown on both sides. Serve with:

Celtic Egg Sauce

¼ cup Squeeze Parkay margarine ¼ cup flour 2 cups milk ¾ teaspoon salt Dash of pepper	3 hard-cooked eggs, chopped 2 tablespoons chopped pimiento 1 tablespoon chopped chives 1 teaspoon Kraft pure prepared mustard

Make a white sauce with margarine, flour, milk and seasonings. Stir in remaining ingredients; heat thoroughly.

6 to 8 servings

Shrimp de Jonghe

1½ cups dry bread crumbs
⅔ cup Squeeze Parkay
   margarine
½ cup dry white wine
⅓ cup chopped parsley

1 garlic clove, minced
½ teaspoon paprika
4½ cups (1½ lbs.) cleaned
   cooked shrimp
2 tablespoons lemon juice

Combine crumbs, margarine, wine, parsley, garlic and paprika. Sprinkle shrimp with juice; toss with approximately ½ cup crumb mixture. Place shrimp in 11¾×7½-inch baking dish; top with remaining crumb mixture. Bake at 400°, 25 minutes.

6 servings

Chili Frank Wrap-Ups

2 cups flour
1 tablespoon baking powder
1 tablespoon chili powder
1 teaspoon salt
1 cup (4 ozs.) shredded Kraft
   sharp natural cheddar
   cheese

2 tablespoons finely chopped
   green pepper
¾ cup milk
⅓ cup Squeeze Parkay
   margarine
10 frankfurters

Combine dry ingredients; stir in cheese and green pepper. Add combined milk and margarine, mixing just until moistened. On lightly floured surface, knead dough about ten times. Roll out dough to 20×10-inch rectangle; cut into ten 5×4-inch rectangles. Place frankfurter on short end of each rectangle; roll up. Seal ends; place on greased cookie sheet. Bake at 450°, 15 minutes.

5 servings

An excellent choice for casual entertaining, especially for the teenage set. Complete the menu with a fresh green salad, a selection of crisp relishes and make-your-own sundaes.

Corny Pizza Handcakes

1 lb. ground beef	½ cup flour
¼ cup chopped onion	½ cup cornmeal
1 8-oz. can tomato sauce	1 tablespoon sugar
1 6-oz. can tomato paste	1 tablespoon baking powder
1 teaspoon salt	1¼ cups milk
½ teaspoon basil leaves	¼ cup Squeeze Parkay
¼ teaspoon oregano leaves	margarine
* * *	1 egg, slightly beaten

Brown meat and onion; drain. Stir in tomato sauce, tomato paste and seasonings. Cover; simmer 15 minutes.

Combine dry ingredients. Add milk, margarine and egg, mixing just until moistened. For each pancake, pour ¼ cup batter onto hot, lightly greased griddle, spreading batter to form a 5½-inch pancake. Cook until surface is bubbly; turn. Continue cooking until golden brown; remove from griddle. Place ¼ cup meat mixture on each pancake; fold in half. Serve immediately.

Approximately 10 servings

To Make Ahead: Place handcakes in 11¾×7½-inch baking dish. Cover tightly; refrigerate. When ready to serve, bake covered at 350°, 35 to 40 minutes or until thoroughly heated.

Handcakes are filled and folded pancakes which are eaten like a sandwich.

Grilled Reuben Sandwiches

Rye bread slices	Corned beef slices
Kraft natural Swiss cheese	Sauerkraut
slices, cut in half	Soft Parkay margarine

For each sandwich, fill two bread slices with cheese, meat and sauerkraut. Spread outside of sandwich with margarine; grill until lightly browned on both sides.

Variation: Before filling sandwiches, spread bread with Kraft thousand island dressing.

Savory Blue Cheese Burgers

⅓ cup soft Parkay margarine
¼ cup Kraft chopped blue
    cheese crumbles
¼ cup finely chopped parsley
1 tablespoon finely chopped
    onion

1 teaspoon Worcestershire
    sauce
¼ teaspoon salt
¼ teaspoon pepper
¼ teaspoon dry mustard
8 hot broiled beef patties
8 hamburger buns, split

Thoroughly blend margarine, cheese, parsley, onion and seasonings. Top each patty with 2 tablespoons margarine mixture; broil until melted. Serve on buns.

8 servings

Variations: Omit hamburger buns; serve burgers open-style on Vienna bread slices or rye bread slices.

Top burgers with tomato slices before adding margarine mixture.

Grilled Ham Salad 'N Cheese

2 cups finely chopped ham
⅓ cup Miracle Whip salad
    dressing
¼ cup sweet pickle relish
16 white bread slices

Kraft pure prepared mustard
16 Kraft American singles
    pasteurized process
    cheese food
Soft Parkay margarine

Combine meat, salad dressing and pickle relish; mix lightly. For each sandwich, spread two bread slices with mustard; cover one bread slice with one process cheese food slice, ham mixture, second process cheese food slice and second bread slice. Spread outside of sandwich with margarine; grill until lightly browned on both sides.

8 sandwiches

Sloppy Joe Grills

½ lb. ground beef
½ cup Kraft barbecue sauce
¼ cup water
2 tablespoons chopped green pepper
2 tablespoons chopped onion

16 white bread slices
1 8-oz. pkg. Kraft pasteurized process American cheese slices
Soft Parkay margarine

Brown meat; drain. Add barbecue sauce, water, green pepper and onion. Simmer 15 minutes. For each sandwich, fill two bread slices with 2 tablespoons meat mixture and process cheese. Spread outside of sandwich with margarine; grill until golden brown on both sides.

8 sandwiches

Variation: Substitute Kraft sharp natural cheddar cheese slices for process cheese slices.

Back To Basics

It's always reassuring to have a few reference recipes readily available for daily meal preparation or entertaining. For your convenience the Kraft Kitchens have compiled a collection of reliable "basics" which includes a variety of sauces, biscuits, muffins, pastry, crumb crusts, doughnuts and pancakes.

Basic Baking Tips

- Read the recipe carefully before beginning.

- Assemble and accurately measure all ingredients.

- Lightly spoon flour into measuring cup, unless the recipe specifies sifting.

- Firmly pack brown sugar into measuring cup.

- All ingredients should be at room temperature, except eggs which are to be separated. Separate eggs while cold, but let egg whites come to room temperature before beating.

- Use large size eggs, whole milk and type of margarine indicated in recipe.

- Thoroughly cream margarine and sugar to blend ingredients and to incorporate air. Room temperature margarine creams easily.

- When adding dry ingredients alternately with liquid ingredients, the first and last additions should be dry ingredients. Thoroughly mix ingredients after each addition.

- When recipe indicates "greased and floured" pan, rub shortening evenly over the pan and sprinkle lightly with flour. Shake out excess flour. Always grease with shortening. Do not use butter, margarine or oil to grease pans.

- Immediately remove cookies and biscuits from cookie sheet.

- Cool baked foods on cooling racks.

- Unfrosted baked items can be securely wrapped in moisture-vaporproof wrap such as aluminum foil and frozen for future use.

Baking Powder Biscuits

2 cups flour
1 tablespoon baking powder
½ teaspoon salt

⅓ cup Parkay margarine
¾ cup milk

Combine dry ingredients; cut in margarine until mixture resembles coarse crumbs. Stir in milk, mixing just until moistened. On lightly floured surface, knead dough ten times. Roll out dough to ½-inch thickness; cut with floured 2-inch cutter. Place on ungreased cookie sheet. Bake at 450°, 10 to 12 minutes or until golden brown.

1½ dozen

Quick Biscuit Mix

6 cups flour
½ cup instant non-fat dry milk
2 tablespoons baking powder

1 tablespoon salt
1½ teaspoons baking soda
1 cup Parkay margarine

Combine dry ingredients; cut in margarine until mixture resembles coarse crumbs. Store in refrigerator in airtight container up to one week.

To Make 1 Dozen Biscuits:
Combine 2½ cups Quick Biscuit Mix and ⅔ cup water, mixing just until moistened. On lightly floured surface, knead dough about ten times. Roll out dough to ½-inch thickness; cut with floured 2½-inch cutter. Place on ungreased cookie sheet. Bake at 450°, 8 to 10 minutes or until golden brown.

Shortcake

2 cups flour
2 tablespoons sugar
1 tablespoon baking powder
½ teaspoon salt

1 egg, slightly beaten
⅔ cup milk
½ cup Parkay margarine,
    melted

Combine dry ingredients. Add combined egg, milk and margarine, mixing just until moistened. Spread into greased and floured 8-inch layer pan. Bake at 450°, 12 to 15 minutes or until golden brown. Cool 10 minutes; remove from pan. Cool; split in half horizontally.

Pancakes

2½ cups flour
  2 tablespoons baking powder
  2 tablespoons sugar
  1 teaspoon salt

2 cups milk
2 eggs, slightly beaten
¼ cup Squeeze Parkay
    margarine

Combine dry ingredients. Add milk, eggs and margarine, mixing just until moistened. For each pancake, pour ¼ cup batter onto hot, lightly greased griddle. Cook until surface is bubbly; turn. Continue cooking until golden brown.

Approximately 1½ dozen

Sourdough Pancakes

1 pkg. active dry yeast
2 cups warm water
4 cups flour
    *   *   *
1 tablespoon sugar

1 teaspoon baking soda
¼ cup milk
1 egg
¼ cup Squeeze Parkay
    margarine

To prepare starter, dissolve yeast in ¼ cup warm water. Combine remaining water and flour. Add yeast; mix well. Cover; let stand at room temperature, 6 hours or overnight.

    Combine sugar and baking soda. Add 2 cups starter, milk, egg and margarine; mix well. For each pancake, pour ¼ cup batter onto hot, lightly greased griddle. Cook until surface is bubbly; turn. Continue cooking until golden brown.

Approximately 1 dozen

Waffles

2 cups flour
4 teaspoons baking powder
1 tablespoon sugar
½ teaspoon salt

2 eggs, slightly beaten
1¾ cups milk
½ cup Squeeze Parkay
    margarine

Combine dry ingredients. Add combined eggs, milk and margarine; mix well. Bake in preheated waffle iron.

6 waffles

Cake Doughnuts

⅓ cup Parkay margarine	1 tablespoon baking powder
⅔ cup sugar	¾ teaspoon salt
4 eggs	1 teaspoon cinnamon
⅓ cup milk	½ teaspoon nutmeg
3 cups flour	Oil

Cream margarine and sugar until light and fluffy. Blend in eggs and milk. Add combined dry ingredients; mix well. Chill. On lightly floured surface, roll out dough to ½-inch thickness; cut with floured doughnut cutter. Let stand 15 minutes. Fry in deep hot oil, 375°, until brown, turning once. Drain on absorbent paper. Coat with sifted confectioners' sugar, if desired.

Approximately 2½ dozen

Cream Puffs

1 cup water	¼ teaspoon salt
½ cup Parkay margarine	4 eggs
1 cup flour	

Bring water and margarine to boil. Add flour and salt; stir vigorously over low heat until mixture forms a ball. Remove from heat. Add eggs, one at a time, beating well after each addition. Drop ¼ cup batter, 3 inches apart, onto ungreased cookie sheet. Bake at 400°, 34 to 40 minutes or until golden brown. Remove from cookie sheet immediately; cool.

1 dozen

Butterscotch Sauce

½ cup packed brown sugar	¼ cup Parkay margarine
½ cup light corn syrup	1 teaspoon vanilla

Combine sugar, corn syrup and margarine; bring to boil, stirring constantly. Continue boiling 1 minute over medium heat, stirring constantly. Remove from heat; stir in vanilla. Serve warm.

1 cup

To Microcook:
Combine sugar, corn syrup and margarine in 1-quart measure. Microcook 4 minutes, stirring after 2 minutes. Stir in vanilla.

Crisp Crust Pastry

1 cup flour
¼ teaspoon salt

⅓ cup Parkay margarine
3 to 4 tablespoons water

Combine flour and salt; cut in margarine until mixture resembles coarse crumbs. Sprinkle with water while mixing lightly with a fork; form into a ball. On lightly floured surface, roll out dough to 12-inch circle. Place in 8 or 9-inch pie plate. Turn and flute edges; prick bottom and sides with fork. Bake at 450°, 10 to 12 minutes or until golden brown.

Note: Recipe may be doubled for a two crust 8 or 9-inch pie.

Vanilla Wafer Crust

1½ cups vanilla wafer crumbs

¼ cup Squeeze Parkay
   margarine

Combine crumbs and margarine; press onto bottom and sides of 9-inch pie plate. Bake at 375°, 8 minutes.

One 9-inch crumb crust

Variation: Substitute chocolate wafer crumbs for vanilla wafer crumbs.

Chocolate Cookie Crust

2 cups (24) crushed
   cream-filled chocolate
   cookies

¼ cup Parkay margarine,
   melted

Combine crumbs and margarine; press onto bottom and sides of 9-inch pie plate. Chill.

One 9-inch crumb crust

Crisp Crust Pastry, Butterscotch Sauce (page 141)

Pastry Pointers

- Handle dough as little as possible when rolling out pastry.
- Roll out dough from center to edge with light, even strokes.
- Lift pastry occasionally to check for sticking.
- Patch an irregular edge or tear by moistening edges of area to be patched and pressing a small piece of pastry firmly in place.
- Don't grease pie plate unless specified.
- Fold rolled-out pastry in half and carefully place in half of pie plate; unfold pastry.
- For single crust pie, trim pastry ½ inch beyond edge of pie plate, fold edge under to make a rim. Flute rim as desired.

Graham Cracker Crust

1¼ cups graham cracker crumbs
¼ cup sugar

¼ cup Squeeze Parkay margarine

Combine crumbs, sugar and margarine; press onto bottom and sides of 9-inch pie plate. Bake at 375°, 8 minutes.

One 9-inch crumb crust

Creamy Frosting

½ cup Parkay margarine
1 teaspoon vanilla
Dash of salt

4½ cups sifted confectioners' sugar
¼ cup milk

Cream margarine; blend in vanilla and salt. Add sugar alternately with milk, beating until light and fluffy.

Frosts two 8 or 9-inch cake layers or one 13×9-inch cake

Single Layer Yellow Cake

⅓ cup Parkay margarine
⅔ cup sugar
1 egg
½ teaspoon vanilla

1 cup flour
1½ teaspoons baking powder
½ teaspoon salt
½ cup milk

Cream margarine and sugar until light and fluffy. Blend in egg and vanilla. Add combined dry ingredients alternately with milk, mixing well after each addition. Pour into greased and floured 8 or 9-inch layer pan. Bake at 350°, 30 to 35 minutes or until wooden pick inserted in center comes out clean. Cool 10 minutes; remove from pan.

Hollandaise Sauce

½ cup Parkay margarine
4 egg yolks
¼ cup water

2 tablespoons lemon juice
Dash of salt and pepper

Melt margarine in double boiler over hot, not boiling, water. Add remaining ingredients; beat constantly at low speed until sauce is thickened.

2 cups

To Microcook:
Microcook margarine in 1-quart measure 45 seconds or until melted. Blend in remaining ingredients. Microcook 1 minute, stirring every 15 seconds. Let stand 4 minutes to thicken.

To Make In A Blender:
Omit water. Place egg yolks, lemon juice and seasonings in blender container; blend on high speed 3 seconds. With blender on high speed, slowly pour in melted margarine. Blend until thickened, about 30 seconds. Serve immediately or heat over warm, not hot, water until ready to serve.

Bran Muffins

2½ cups 40% bran flakes
1¼ cups milk
⅓ cup soft Parkay margarine
1 egg

1¼ cups flour
½ cup sugar
1 tablespoon baking powder
½ teaspoon salt

Combine bran flakes and milk; let stand until cereal softens. Add margarine and egg; mix well. Add combined dry ingredients, mixing just until moistened. Spoon into greased medium-size muffin pan, filling each cup ⅔ full. Bake at 400°, 25 minutes.

1 dozen

Old-Fashioned Sugar Cookies

1 cup Parkay margarine
Sugar
2 eggs
½ teaspoon vanilla

3½ cups flour
½ teaspoon baking powder
½ teaspoon baking soda
½ teaspoon salt

Cream margarine and 1 cup sugar until light and fluffy. Blend in eggs and vanilla. Add combined dry ingredients; mix well. Chill. On lightly floured surface, roll out dough to ⅛-inch thickness; cut with assorted 2½-inch cutters. Place on ungreased cookie sheet; sprinkle with sugar. Bake at 400°, 6 to 8 minutes or until edges are lightly browned.

Approximately 6 dozen

Variation: Sprinkle dough with colored sugar or cinnamon-sugar before baking.

SUGAR · ALLSPICE · CINNAMON

Medium White Sauce

¼ cup Parkay margarine
¼ cup flour
½ teaspoon salt

Dash of pepper
2 cups milk

Melt margarine in saucepan over low heat. Blend in flour and seasonings. Gradually add milk; cook, stirring constantly, until thickened.

2¼ cups

Variations: For thin white sauce, decrease margarine and flour to 2 tablespoons each.

For thick white sauce, increase margarine and flour to 6 tablespoons each.

Lemon Chive Sauce

½ cup Squeeze Parkay margarine
3 tablespoons lemon juice

1 tablespoon chopped chives
2 teaspoons grated lemon rind

Combine ingredients. Serve hot or cold with fish.

Approximately ¾ cup

Béarnaise Sauce

½ cup Parkay margarine
3 egg yolks
2 tablespoons water

1 tablespoon white vinegar
1 tablespoon finely chopped
  green onion

Melt margarine in double boiler over hot, not boiling, water. Add remaining ingredients; beat constantly with electric or rotary beater at low speed until sauce is thickened.

1½ cups

Cheddar Cheese Sauce

¼ cup Parkay margarine
¼ cup flour
½ teaspoon salt
Dash of cayenne
Dash of dry mustard

2 cups milk
2 cups (8 ozs.) shredded
Kraft sharp natural
cheddar cheese

Melt margarine in saucepan over low heat. Blend in flour and seasonings. Gradually add milk; cook, stirring constantly, until thickened. Add cheese; stir until melted.

2⅔ cups

Variation: Add 2 tablespoons chopped parsley, green pepper or green onion.

Sunny Citrus Sauce

½ cup sugar
1 tablespoon cornstarch
Dash of salt
1 cup water

⅓ cup Parkay margarine
2 tablespoons lemon juice
1 teaspoon grated lemon
rind

Combine sugar, cornstarch and salt in saucepan; gradually add water. Cook over medium heat, stirring constantly, until thickened. Remove from heat; blend in margarine, lemon juice and lemon rind. Serve hot or cold.

1½ cups

Hard Sauce

½ cup Parkay margarine
1 teaspoon vanilla

2 cups sifted confectioners'
sugar

Cream margarine; blend in vanilla. Add sugar, beating until light and fluffy.

1⅓ cups

Variations: Substitute 1 teaspoon grated lemon or orange rind for vanilla.

Substitute 1 teaspoon rum flavoring for vanilla.

INGREDIENT SUBSTITUTIONS

1 teaspoon baking powder	¼ teaspoon baking soda plus ½ teaspoon cream of tartar
1 cup cake flour	1 cup minus 2 tablespoons all-purpose flour
1 oz. unsweetened chocolate	3 tablespoons cocoa plus 1 tablespoon margarine
1 tablespoon cornstarch	2 tablespoons flour or 4 teaspoons quick-cooking tapioca
1 cup light cream	⅞ cup milk plus 3 tablespoons margarine
1 cup heavy cream (except for whipping)	¾ cup milk plus ⅓ cup margarine
1 egg	2 egg yolks plus 1 tablespoon water or 2 egg yolks (for custard)
1 cup honey	1¼ cups sugar plus ¼ cup liquid
1 cup fresh whole milk	½ cup evaporated milk plus ½ cup water or 1 cup reconstituted non-fat dry milk plus 2 teaspoons margarine
1 cup sour milk or buttermilk	1 tablespoon lemon juice or vinegar plus milk to make 1 cup (let stand 5 minutes)
¼ cup chopped fresh onion	1 tablespoon instant minced onion, rehydrated
1 cake compressed yeast	1 package or 2 teaspoons active dry yeast

COOKING TERMS

Baste: Spoon liquid over meat or other foods during cooking to add flavor and prevent drying of the surface. The liquid may be melted margarine, meat drippings or sauce.

Beat: Thoroughly combine ingredients and incorporate air with a rapid, regular motion.

Blend: Thoroughly combine two or more ingredients or prepare food in an electric blender.

Chill: Refrigerate until cold.

Chop: Cut into pieces of random size.

Coat: Cover surface of food evenly.

Cool: Allow to come to room temperature.

Cream: Soften margarine, by beating with a spoon or mixer. This usually refers to blending a sugar and a fat together.

Cube: Cut into pieces of uniform size and shape, usually ½ inch or larger.

Cut In: Combine margarine with dry ingredients by using a pastry blender or two knives in a scissor motion until particles are of desired size — i.e., coarse crumbs.

Dash: Add less than ⅛ teaspoon of an ingredient.

Dot: Evenly distribute small amounts of an ingredient such as margarine.

Fold In: Combine delicate ingredients such as beaten egg whites or whipped cream with other ingredients. Gently cut down through the center of the mixture, across the bottom of the bowl, up and over the top of the mixture, using a circular motion.

Grease: Rub shortening (not butter, margarine or oil) on surface of pan or dish to prevent sticking.

Heavy Cream: Cream that has a fat content of at least 36% and is generally used for whipping. Heavy cream is often referred to as whipping cream.

Knead: Work dough with a press-and-fold motion to evenly distribute ingredients and develop texture. Flatten the ball of dough and fold in half toward you. Press and push away with the heel of your hand. Rotate dough a quarter turn and repeat process until dough surface is smooth.

Mixing Just Until Moistened: Combine ingredients for a batter or dough until dry ingredients are thoroughly moistened, but mixture is still lumpy.

Packed Brown Sugar: Fill measure by pressing with a spoon. Sugar will hold its shape when inverted from the measure.

Rounded Teaspoonful: Measurement for dough, as for cookies, slightly mounded in a flatware (not measuring) teaspoon.

Sauté: Brown or cook in a small amount of hot fat.

Shred: Cut into very thin pieces using a shredder or knife.

Soft Peaks: Stage in beating egg whites when mixture will form soft rounded peaks when beaters are removed.

Stiff Peaks: Stage in beating egg whites when mixture will hold stiff pointed peaks when beaters are removed. The mixture is glossy, not dry.

Stir-fry: Cook in small amount of margarine over medium to high heat, stirring continuously until ingredients are tender, yet crisp.

Whip: Beat rapidly with a wire whisk, rotary beater or electric mixer to incorporate air and increase volume.

White Sauce: Basic sauce made with margarine, flour, seasonings and milk. Melt margarine in saucepan over low heat. Blend in flour and seasonings. Gradually add milk; cook, stirring constantly, until thickened.

Index

154

160